TO:

....

FROM:

....

DATE:

....

IN
God's
IMAGE

100 DEVOTIONS
FOR MEN

DAVID SANFORD

BARBOUR
PUBLISHING

ISBN 978-1-63609-148-8

Published by Barbour Publishing, Inc., 1810 Barbour Drive, Uhrichsville, Ohio 44683, www.barbourbooks.com

Our mission is to inspire the world with the life-changing message of the Bible.

Member of the
Evangelical Christian
Publishers Association

Printed in China.

WHAT DOES IT MEAN TO BE MADE *"in God's image"?*

It means you can influence your world for good. In the very first chapter of scripture, God says, "Let us make man in our image, after our likeness" (Genesis 1:26 KJV). Though every human being bears God's image, this powerful devotional focuses on men in particular.

You can and should reflect God's image as you

- work, create, provide, and protect
- love, teach, confront, and forgive
- guide, help, encourage, and sacrifice

One hundred readings are based on scriptures that show God in action, exhibiting the positive and beneficial characteristics that men, made in His image, are blessed to follow.

Here is challenge and encouragement for Christian men in a world that desperately needs them. . .that needs *you!*

THE MAGNITUDE OF GOD'S GREAT GOODNESS

"They reveled in your [God's] great goodness."
NEHEMIAH 9:25

God is *great*. God is *good*. He wants you to know and love Him. And then the one true Lord God wants you to be His hands and feet here on earth.

Don't worry. It's not hard. Actually, a lot of what we'll explore in this book will spark smiles, joy, and even fun. That's the way God designed it. And for that we can be glad!

Let's start with who God is. Again, He is *great* and *good*.

The Lord God spoke the heavens and earth into existence. This was the first physical manifestation of the Trinity's plan from all eternity past. It resoundingly proves how *great* God is.

Then the Lord God created every living thing on earth.

Last of all, He made man from the dust of the earth and breathed the breath of life into him. Man was a living soul with a spirit attuned to his Creator.

All this resoundingly proves how *good* God is.

Yes, God is infinite and eternal, and we are not. But God gladly imparts to us a small portion of His infinite, eternal being.

To be born is to be tagged "Made by God in His Image." True, sin mars that image. Then again, that's what God's Son and Holy Spirit remake.

We'll cover this further in coming pages. For now, simply remember: First, God is *great* and *good*. Second, God wants you to know and love Him. Third, God wants you to be His hands and feet here on earth.

God, I feel Your delight as I begin this new devotional book. Thank You so much for putting it in my hands. Spark smiles, joy, and fun in and through me. Amen!

THE MAJESTY
OF GOD'S IMAGE

*Then God said, "Let us make mankind
in our image, in our likeness."*
Genesis 1:26

God is *infinite*. God is *eternal*. And He is so much more.
We can never begin to understand the magnitude of
His greatness and goodness.

Everything God is, He has been from eternity past,
and He will be for all eternity future. Among other things,
He is always all-powerful (omnipotent), everywhere-
present (omnipresent), and everything-knowing
(omniscient).

What's more, the one true Lord God is a *Trinity* of
three equal, infinite, and eternal persons: God the Father,
God the Son (Jesus Christ), and God the Holy Spirit.

All the fullness of God's greatness and goodness
resides in each person of the Trinity. The Father isn't
smarter than the Son. The Son isn't stronger than the

Spirit. They're never in conflict. They never have two-to-one votes. Instead, they enjoy perfect harmony.

When we read about God, Jesus, or the Holy Spirit in the Bible, we always want to "see" the Trinity. This is true in Genesis 1:1-2, which mentions God and the Spirit. Rest assured God's Son was actively involved!

Then again, it's easy to see God the Father ("This is my Son, whom I love") and the Holy Spirit (descending as a dove) both actively involved in the baptism of God's Son, Jesus. They celebrated again in the Mount of Transfiguration and in Jesus Christ's bodily resurrection from the dead.

As we saw yesterday, to be born is to be tagged "Made by God in His Image." While we will never be fully free from sin, God is in the process of transforming us.

For now, simply remember: First, God is *infinite*. Second, God is *eternal*. Third, God is a *Trinity* of three equal and harmonious persons.

And, you bear the Trinity's image!

God, thank You for making me in Your image. Now, please make me Your hands and feet here on earth.

THREE WAYS WE'RE MADE IN GOD'S IMAGE

The light of the gospel. . .displays the glory of Christ, who is the image of God.
2 CORINTHIANS 4:4

God *made* us. That's creation. God's *remaking* us. That's transformation!

Before creation, God's Son, Jesus Christ, knew that one day (Christmas) He would be not only fully God but also become fully man. Even now in heaven He has a glorified human body. And the Holy Spirit knew that one day (Pentecost) He would reside in every follower of Jesus Christ. Even now He resides in us!

So, to say that we're made in God's image doesn't simply mean that we're sons of Adam, that is, descendants of the first man God created out of the dust of the earth.

Instead, it also means that we were created by God to follow and become like His Son, Jesus Christ, and one day enjoy glorified human bodies in heaven and in the new heavens and new earth. What's more, it means that we have God's Holy Spirit residing in us to empower that Christ-like transformation.

It all starts with becoming a child of God.

Yes, sin marred God's image in humanity. Then again, Jesus Christ lived a perfect life, took on all the sin of everyone for all of history in His own body, was nailed to a cruel Roman cross, died for us and for our sins, was buried, and physically rose again on the third day.

As a result, God gets all the credit, honor, and praise for making and remaking us in His image. He imparts a small part of His infinite, eternal being into us at salvation in Jesus Christ and through the Holy Spirit residing in us.

Never forget: Even a tiny part of God's infinite and eternal nature is more than enough.

God, thank You so much for saving me and now remaking me. What a great plan.

GOD'S IMAGE IS
SO MUCH GREATER

*"The God who made the world and everything in it
is the Lord of heaven and earth and does not live in
temples built by human hands. And he is not served
by human hands, as if he needed anything. Rather, he
himself gives everyone life and breath and everything
else. From one man he made all the nations, that they
should inhabit the whole earth; and he marked out
their appointed times in history and the boundaries of
their lands. God did this so that they would seek him
and perhaps reach out for him."*

ACTS 17:24–27

So far, we've seen that God is *great* and *good*. As a
result, God wants you to know and love Him. And then
the one true Lord God wants you to be His hands and
feet here on earth.

Second, we've seen that God is *infinite* and *eternal*.
And God is so much more. We can never begin to

understand the magnitude of His greatness and goodness.

In addition, we've seen that God is a *Trinity* of three equal, infinite, and eternal persons: God the Father, God the Son (Jesus Christ), and God the Holy Spirit.

What's more, we've seen that God *made* us. That's creation. And God's *remaking* us. That's transformation—into His image.

Our response?

We want to thank God daily for who He is!

We can thank the Lord for everything about Him. This includes His sovereignty (greatness), providence (goodness and guidance), holiness (glory), love (graciousness), and mystery ("only God knows").

We've covered a lot of ground, but much more could be said about God. That's why Bible reading is so important.

On the next few pages, we'll specifically see more about what the New Testament says about God's Son and Holy Spirit.

God, thank You so much for who You are! Now more than ever, I'm so glad to be made in Your image. Please keep remaking me thanks to Your Spirit and Your Son.

JESUS CHRIST IS GOD'S PERFECT IMAGE

When all the people were being baptized, Jesus was baptized too. And as he was praying, heaven was opened and the Holy Spirit descended on him in bodily form like a dove. And [God the Father's] voice came from heaven: "You are my Son, whom I love; with you I am well pleased."

LUKE 3:21–22

Jesus Christ is fully God and two thousand years ago became fully human. God now is remaking us in the image of His Son. This brings great joy to the Trinity!

John 1:14 says, "The Word [Jesus] became flesh and made his dwelling among us. We have seen his glory, the glory of the one and only Son, who came from the Father, full of grace and truth."

John 1:18 adds, "No one has ever seen God, but the one and only Son [Jesus,] who is himself God and is in closest relationship with the Father, has made him known."

Colossians 1:15–16 says, "The Son is the image of the invisible God. . . . For in him [Jesus] all things were created: things in heaven and on earth, visible and invisible, whether thrones or powers or rulers or authorities; all things have been created through him and for him."

And Hebrews 1:2–3 tells us, "In these last days he [God the Father] has spoken to us by his Son, whom he appointed heir of all things, and through whom also he made the universe. The Son is the radiance of God's glory and the exact representation of his being, sustaining all things by his powerful word. After he had provided purification for sins, he sat down at the right hand of the Majesty in heaven."

Praise God for His Son, Jesus Christ.

God, I thank You that Jesus is Your perfect image made visible. Now, You are remaking me to be Your hands and feet. Amen.

THE HOLY SPIRIT
IS REMAKING US

We speak without fear because our trust is in Christ. . . . The heart is free where the Spirit of the Lord is. The Lord is the Spirit. . . . All the time we are being changed to look like Him, with more and more of His shining-greatness. This change is from the Lord Who is the Spirit.

2 CORINTHIANS 3:12, 17–18 NLV

The Spirit and water appear repeatedly in scripture. From the earliest part of Genesis (1:2) to the final portion of Revelation (22:17), we see water and the Holy Spirit poured into humankind, people who are made in God's image.

Isaiah 44:3 gives this promise: "For I [the Lord] will pour water on the thirsty land, and streams on the dry ground; I will pour out my Spirit on your offspring, and my blessing on your descendants."

And John 1:33 indicates that promise's fulfillment

isn't far away. "The one who sent me [John the Baptist] to baptize with water told me, 'The man on whom you see the Spirit come down and remain is the one who will baptize with the Holy Spirit.'"

In Acts 1:5, Jesus announced that promise's fulfillment would happen *very* soon: "For John baptized with water, but in a few days you will be baptized with the Holy Spirit."

Everyone who trusts Jesus Christ receives a tremendous gift immediately. That gift is God pouring His Spirit into us to remake us. His holiness, courage, wisdom, power, truthfulness, and much more now fill our lives!

God, I want to experience, and overflow with a renewal of Your Holy Spirit, especially Your love, joy, peace, forbearance, kindness, goodness, faithfulness, gentleness, and self-control (Galatians 5:22–23).

WE ARE GOD'S HANDS AND FEET

"Look at My hands and My feet. See! It is I, Myself!
Touch Me and see for yourself. A spirit does not
have flesh and bones as I have." When Jesus had
said this, He showed them His hands and feet.

LUKE 24:39–40 NLV

Only a few days after Jesus Christ's ascension, God poured out His Holy Spirit on all His followers. And He's continued to pour out the Spirit on all new believers ever since. This is one of the great mysteries of the faith.

First Timothy 3:16 reminds us: "Beyond all question, *the mystery from which true godliness springs is great:* He [Jesus] appeared in the flesh, was vindicated by the Spirit, was seen by angels, was preached among the nations, was believed on in the world, was taken up in glory" (emphasis added).

As spirit-filled Christian men today, we can reflect God's image in dozens of ways. Those ways include as we work, create, provide, and protect; as we love, teach, confront, and forgive; and as we guide, help, encourage, and sacrifice.

We also reflect God's image as we celebrate, cherish, clothe, and comfort; as we enjoy, feed, give, and honor; and as we pray, provide, speak, and treasure.

As we reflect God's image, *we* are blessed, *others* are blessed, and the *world* is influenced for good and for God's glory, honor, and praise. What's more, over the next three months, you'll deepen your appreciation for who God made you.

There's nothing more exciting, invigorating, and fulfilling than becoming more like your Lord and Savior and more fully owning your identity as "Made by God in His Image."

Get ready to experience promised smiles, joy, and even fun!

God, I'm ready! Use me as Your hands and feet.

WE WORK HEARTILY

Whatever work you do, do it with all your heart. Do it for the Lord and not for men. Remember that you will get your reward from the Lord. He will give you what you should receive. You are working for the Lord Christ.
<small>COLOSSIANS 3:23–24 NLV</small>

God is not afraid of hard work. He created the whole universe, after all. Furthermore, Jesus worked hard six days a week for two decades. Again, the Lord is not afraid of hard work!

As men "Made by God In His Image," we're designed to work hard. It pleases God, fulfills us and—when done for the Lord—earns eternal rewards.

Jesus and many others in scripture worked heartily and wholeheartedly.

The Bible repeatedly honors Joshua's right hand man, Caleb, for serving the Lord "wholeheartedly" (Numbers 14:24, 32:12, Deuteronomy 1:36, and Joshua

14:9 and 14:14). King Hezekiah, too, is noted for serving the Lord wholeheartedly: "In all that he did in the service of the Temple of God and in his efforts to follow God's laws and commands, Hezekiah sought his God wholeheartedly. As a result, he was very successful" (2 Chronicles 31:21 NLT; see also 2 Kings 20:3 and Isaiah 38:3).

Echoing today's scripture above, the apostle Paul went on to tell servants: "Obey [your masters] not only to win their favor when their eye is on you, but as slaves of Christ, doing the will of God from your heart" (Ephesians 6:6). As is always the case with service to God, there is a reward. Paul continues, "Serve wholeheartedly, as if you were serving the Lord, not people, because you know that the Lord will reward each one for whatever good they do, whether they are slave or free" (Ephesians 6:7–8).

We honor the God who made us in His own image by working hard. What job should you be doing today?

God, You give me the strength and desire to work hard. Now direct me to the job You want me to accomplish. Use me as You see fit.

WE REST FROM OUR WORK

"Work may be done for six days. But the seventh day is a Day of Rest, holy to the Lord."
EXODUS 31:15 NLV

The theme of resting from work is found all through scripture, from Genesis to Revelation.

God rested from His work. We see this in Genesis 2:2–3 (NLT), which says, "On the seventh day God had finished his work of creation, so he rested from all his work. And God blessed the seventh day and declared it holy, because it was the day when he rested from all his work of creation." (See also Hebrews 4:4.)

God commanded us to rest from work. Exodus 20:10 (NLT) makes this abundantly clear: "The seventh day is a Sabbath day of rest dedicated to the LORD your God. On that day no one in your household may do any work. This includes you, your sons and daughters, your male and female servants, your livestock, and any foreigners living among you" (see also today's key verse and Exodus 23:12, 35:2, Leviticus 23:3, and Deuteronomy 5:14).

God blesses us when we rest from work. Psalm 127:2 (NLT) tells us, "It is useless for you to work so hard from early morning until late at night, anxiously working for food to eat; for God gives rest to his loved ones."

God promises an eternal rest. In Revelation 14:13 (NLT), John reports that he "heard a voice from heaven saying, 'Write this down: Blessed are those who die in the Lord from now on. Yes, says the Spirit, they are blessed indeed, for they will rest from their hard work; for their good deeds follow them!'"

Christian men have no obligation to work themselves to the bone. If God Himself "rested" from His work, the guys He made in His image should too. Be sure to insert some Sabbath times into your schedule. You (and God) will be pleased!

Lord, You designed us to rest each night, and to take off one day each week. Please help me to calm my mind and body to get the rest I need.

WE REST IN GOD'S JOY

They rested and made it a day of feasting and joy.
ESTHER 9:17

In Bible times, God's people had numerous opportunities to take a day off work and celebrate with a feast. There were Sabbath days, monthly and annual holy days, birthdays, weddings, circumcisions, dedications, weanings, harvest times, the arrival of out of town guests, and even the return of prodigals (Luke 15:20-24).

Jewish families were instructed to invite Levites, widows, orphans, foreigners, the crippled, and the poor to help them celebrate each feast. Most took place in homes, but the three most important ones took place in Jerusalem. These were times for great joy!

No one seemed to attend more feasts than Jesus Himself. He enjoyed opportunities to meet new people and whet their appetites for the Kingdom of God. No surprise: His first miracle was at a wedding feast (John 2).

In His preaching and teaching, Jesus spoke of the feast in the kingdom of heaven and how great it will be for those who accept His invitation (Matthew 8:11, Luke 13:29, 14:16-24; see also Isaiah 25:6). Jesus also used banquets as the settings for many of His parables.

When is the last time you hosted a banquet? Or accepted an invitation to someone else's feast? A good, wholesome party is more Christlike than you may have realized. As you celebrate, keep this motto clearly in mind: "Have fun and share joy!" Make it easy for others to ask the reason for your winsome, irresistible happiness. You can tell them you're simply reflecting the joy of the God in whose image you're made.

Lord God, prompt me to celebrate the happy events of this life with joy—Your joy. May I rest in Your joy and encourage others to do the same.

WE REST IN GOD'S PEACE

*He lets me rest in green meadows; he leads
me beside peaceful streams.*
PSALM 23:2 NLT

Besides resting in peace after death (Genesis 15:15, 2 Kings 20:19, Job 3:13 and Isaiah 57:2), the Bible describes other ways to enjoy or rest in God's peace.

The first is enjoyed by people and their rulers in the absence of war and the abundance of God's provision. This was the case for years under Othniel (Judges 3:11), Ehud (Judges 3:30), Deborah and Barak (Judges 5:31), Gideon (Judges 8:28), Solomon (1 Chronicles 22:9), Asa (2 Chronicles 14:1-7), Jehoshaphat (2 Chronicles 20:30), and Hezekiah (2 Kings 20:19 and Isaiah 39:8). This is God's desire for all His people (see today's scripture plus Psalm 147:14, Proverbs 3:2, Isaiah 32:18, and 1 Timothy 2:2).

The second way to rest in God's peace is offered by Jesus Christ. This is true in His followers' lives now, and it will be universally true during His millennial reign (Luke 2:14 and 19:42, Acts 10:36, Colossians 1:20 and Revelation 20:4-6). Jesus is the embodiment of God's rest and peace for His people (Isaiah 9:6-7, 26:3, 53:5).

The third description of resting in God's peace involves godly Christian men from the time of the apostles (Matthew 10:11-13 and Luke 10:5-6) up through the present time (Matthew 5:9, John 14:27, Romans 12:18, 14:19, and James 3:18).

The fourth includes our sincerely blessing others practically, then saying the words, "Go in peace" (Mark 5:34, Luke 7:50, 8:48, John 20:21, Acts 15:33, 16:36, and James 2:16). This applies to fellow Christians and not-yet-Christians alike.

Our God is a God of peace (Romans 16:20, Philippians 4:9, 1 Thessalonians 5:23, and Hebrews 13:20). As men made in His image, we can know this peace personally and share it with others.

God, make me a Christian man who exhibits, shares, and speaks words of peace to everyone around me.

WE REST IN GOD'S PRESENCE

The LORD replied, "My Presence will
go with you, and I will give you rest."
EXODUS 33:14

The man who doesn't want God's presence above all else ends up losing that "all else." Think of Adam in Genesis 3.

Conversely, the man who wants God's presence more than anything else enjoys God's presence throughout his life. Think of two princes of Egypt—Joseph in Genesis 39-50 and Moses in the book of Exodus and Psalm 90.

True, Joseph and Moses went through a lot of trials and tribulations. But they ended up becoming two of the greatest men in biblical history. That wouldn't have been possible without a deep, abiding sense of God's presence in their lives.

In their lives and the lives of others, scripture shows us that hope can come out of deep pain. Out of deep pain can come a much richer sense of God's purposeful guidance and provision. Out of deep pain can come a bridge to one's God-given destiny.

Jesus left His most important words for last: "And surely I am with you always, to the very end of the age" (Matthew 28:20).

Is that your experience? If yes, great! If no, lift up this heartfelt prayer: "God, I want to sense Your presence."

This is a prayer God will gladly answer, though He may do so through trials. Knowing that you are made in His image, and that His desire is to conform you ever closer to that image (specifically of His Son, Jesus Christ, Romans 8:29), you can rest in His presence.

There is never need to fret.

God, I want Your presence. I echo Joseph and Moses and the psalm writers: I need You with me. Please help me sense Your presence today.

WE ACT RIGHTEOUSLY

"Seek the Kingdom of God above all
else, and live righteously, and he will
give you everything you need."
MATTHEW 6:33 NLT

Like every other virtue, righteousness originates with the Lord God. His righteousness is infinite and eternal, yet He gives a small part of it to His people. As a result, God's people can act righteously.

Of course, that assumes those people aren't doing what is "right" in their own eyes (Judges 17:6 and 21:25).

Instead, it assumes God's men are doing what is right in the sight of the Lord (1 Kings 14:8, 15:5, and 22:43; as well as 2 Kings 12:2, 14:3, 15:3, 15:34, 18:3, and 22:2).

Ultimately, God's righteous men live by faith and live faithfully in God's eyes (Ezekiel 18:9, Habakkuk 2:4, Romans 1:17, 2 Corinthians 5:7, Galatians 2:20, 3:11, 2 Timothy 1:5, and Hebrews 10:38).

That doesn't mean we act righteously 100 percent of the time. In heaven, however, we have an advocate, "Jesus Christ the righteous" (1 John 2:1 KJV).

My mentor Luis Palau, the international evangelist, said it well: "Keep short accounts with God and others . . . . Allow the Holy Spirit to shine His divine spotlight in your heart. Let Him clean out every room in your soul. Then claim God's wonderful promises."

One of God's wonderful promises says, "If we confess our sins, he [God] is faithful and just and will forgive us our sins and *purify us from all unrighteousness*" (1 John 1:9, emphasis added).

Another wonderful promise appears in the second half of today's key verse above.

What great promises, indeed!

God, I want to be a man who does what is right
in Your sight. I want to live by faith, faithfully.
I confess my unrighteousness. Thank You for
forgiveness of my sins through Jesus Christ.
May I act righteously today. Amen.

WE CONFRONT TRUTHFULLY

"Now then, stand here, because I [Samuel] am going to confront you with evidence before the LORD as to all the righteous acts performed by the LORD for you."
1 SAMUEL 12:7

While reading the Bible, have you ever winced, maybe even shaken your head, when a hero of the faith isn't "nice"? How about when you read today's scripture? "I am going to confront you" certainly doesn't sound nice. Could we be missing the point of the scripture passages that make us cringe?

Check every major English-language Bible published in the past five centuries. Stick with the biblical text itself. The word "nice" doesn't appear once. We need to open up to the Holy Spirit's leading to be more than a "nice, loving Christian brother" when we need to confront a fellow believer. While "loving Christian brother" is essential, "nice" doesn't accurately describe what God the Father, Jesus Christ, and the Spirit have in mind.

Author Randy Alcorn says: "We've been schooled that it's inappropriate to say anything negative. . . . We've redefined 'Christlike' to mean 'nice.' " Alcorn is right on the mark. What a mistake.

Then again, God doesn't ask us to serve as judge, jury, and executioner. Instead, He asks us to confirm the facts and then go to our Christian brother, ask questions, listen, and speak the truth in love. The goal isn't merely conviction of sin, but repentance before God (Proverbs 28:13).

Thankfully, God promises to forgive all who repent from their sins and turn back to Him (1 John 1:9). May we reflect His image by faithfully pointing everyone to Him. As the apostle Peter tells us, God is "not willing that any should perish, but that all should come to repentance" (2 Peter 3:9 KJV).

God, I'd rather not confront anyone else yet. Instead, I need to confront my own sins. Cleanse me, forgive me, and make me a vessel of honor available for Your use.

WE GIVE GRACE

*May God our Father and the Lord Jesus
Christ give you grace and peace.*
ROMANS 1:7 NLT (SEE ALSO 1 CORINTHIANS 1:3, 2
CORINTHIANS 1:2, GALATIANS 1:3, EPHESIANS 1:2,
PHILIPPIANS 1:2, 2 THESSALONIANS 1:2, TITUS 1:4,
AND PHILEMON 3)

If you lived at the time of the apostles, saying grace wasn't simply something you did over meals. Instead, it was something you prayed over all your Christian brothers (Titus 3:15).

The beginning of every epistle by Paul begins with a prayer for God to grant His grace to the readers. That includes the nine listed above plus Colossians 1:2, 1 Thessalonians 1:1, 1 Timothy 1:2, 2 Timothy 1:2. Ditto some of the non-Paul letters: 1 Peter 1:2 and 2 Peter 1:2, and 2 John 3. That's sixteen of the twenty-one New Testament epistles.

What's more, in Bible times you "said grace" to

explain God's blessings in your life (Genesis 33:5, Ezra 7:6, Nehemiah 2:8, Psalm 84:11, and Acts 20:32). You pointed to God's grace as the source of the spiritual gifts He gave you for building up others (Romans 12:6, 1 Corinthians 1:4, and Ephesians 3:7). And you credited God for giving you grace by His answers to your specific prayers (2 Corinthians 1:11 and 9:14).

Grace is clearly an aspect of God, and something that should be part of His children, who are made in His image. Be aware, though, that God gives His grace only to the humble (James 4:6 and 1 Peter 5:5). Humility is the trademark, therefore, of Christians who receive God's grace and credit Him for giving His abundant grace to them.

How often do you say, in effect, "Thank God for His grace"?

Are you humble and grateful enough to say grace to someone else today?

God, Your gracious giving accounts for everything good I enjoy. I don't deserve any of it. But I praise You. Help me to say grace over someone today.

WE GIVE MERCY

*May God the Father and Christ Jesus our
Lord give you grace, mercy, and peace.*
1 TIMOTHY 1:2, 2 TIMOTHY 1:2 NLT

Like the epistles of 2 John and Jude, Paul's letters to Timothy each begin with a prayer for God to grant mercy. After peace and grace, mercy was the third most common blessing to pray for one's brothers and sisters in Jesus Christ.

James gave thanks "for the Lord is full of tenderness and mercy" (James 5:11 NLT). In essence, he echoed Jeremiah, who wrote, "It is of the LORD's mercies that we are not consumed, because his compassions fail not" (Lamentations 3:22 KJV).

If anyone wonders about the classic accounts of God's mercy—shown to Adam and Eve, Noah and his family, Abraham and Lot, Isaiah in his vision of heaven, Jonah in the great fish—all we have to do is see what Jesus said. He cited them all.

This includes a classic Bible story Jesus mentioned in His first recorded sermon. He was preaching in His hometown synagogue. Partway through that sermon, Jesus said: "There were many in Israel with leprosy in the time of Elisha the prophet, yet not one of them was cleansed—only Naaman the Syrian" (Luke 4:27; see also 2 Kings 5:1–15).

So, what point was Jesus making? "God extends His mercy to *His* worst enemies—and to *ours*," says Rob Heijermans. That idea was radical enough to cause the synagogue crowd to instantly riot, drive Jesus to a nearby cliff, and try to toss the Messiah to His death.

In other words, God extends mercy to us—we relish that. Extending mercy to our worst enemies—we rage against that. An unnamed Jewish slave girl who relished the God of Israel's mercy, demonstrated it to her cruel master, Naaman, shows us another way.

We reflect God's image when we show mercy to others as He shows it to us.

God, it's hard to extend Your mercy to my enemies. Show me how to do so.

WE GIVE STRENGTH

*For the eyes of the LORD run to and fro throughout
the whole earth, to shew himself strong in the behalf
of them whose heart is perfect toward him.*

2 CHRONICLES 16:9 KJV

One of the first men who found favor in the Lord's eyes
was Noah (Genesis 6:8). One of the first new names
for the Lord is the Living One, God, "who sees me"
(Genesis 16:13–14).

One of the Bible's great heroes, David, actively de-
sired to receive valor, strength, and protection because
of the Lord's eyes on him (1 Samuel 26:24). David knew
his future depended on finding favor in the Lord's eyes
(2 Samuel 15:25). Years later, it was said that David did
what was right in the Lord's eyes, "save only in the
matter of Uriah the Hittite" (1 Kings 15:5 KJV). Other
kings were judged by whether or not they had done
right in the Lord's eyes.

Some kings, like David, sinned greatly, but then

repented and received forgiveness. Others, like Solomon, appeared to be fully committed to the Lord but proved to be only half-hearted. These men sinned, didn't repent, and became no-hearted. Still others were no-hearted from start to finish. Only one king, Jotham, apparently avoided great sin and didn't need to repent in a big way (2 Kings 15:34 and 2 Chronicles 27:2).

No wonder the eyes of the Lord search the whole earth (see today's scripture and Zechariah 4:10).

We sometimes forget that the Lord God is wholehearted in every positive and beneficial characteristic. He is never half-hearted or no-hearted (and thus capricious) toward us as individuals, the rest of humanity, the earth, or the universe. Phew!

As men made in God's image, we're designed to be wholehearted and fully committed to Him. If we are, we become men filled and overflowing with God's power and strength. . .and we can pass that along to others.

Lord, I want to be fully committed to
You and overflowing with Your strength.
May Your power change the magnitudes
of my love, courage, and prayers.

WE CREATE FROM WHAT GOD CREATED

By faith we understand that the universe was formed at God's command, so that what is seen was not made out of what was visible.
HEBREWS 11:3

All men are creators. You don't have to be a painter, novelist, or filmmaker to be considered "creative." Maybe you cook some incredible chili or put up the best Christmas display in the neighborhood or find clever ways to repair a rusted tailpipe.

Opportunities for creativity are endless because we get the creative urge from our infinite God. Of course, there is a big difference between God's *primary* and our *secondary* creativity, as illustrated by an old joke. . . .

An eminent scientist and his colleagues go outside.

The scientist looks around, calls out to God, and says, "Our knowledge has advanced to the point at which we don't need You anymore. We've built automobiles, harnessed the atom, and flown to the moon. Now we're ready to create a new kind of man in our own image."

"Really?" God says. "Show Me."

The scientist kneels, scoops some dirt, and begins to form a man.

"Hey, wait a minute," God tells him. "You need to start with your *own* dirt."

Yes, God is the source of everything. In turn, He encourages us to combine and manipulate our world's raw materials in ways that benefit ourselves and other people. That's implied in His command to mankind to subdue the earth (Genesis 1:28). Only a few pages later, God highlights a man named Tubal-Cain, "who forged all kinds of tools out of bronze and iron" (4:22).

We are creative because God is creative. And when you apply your own creativity to beneficial ends, you honor the God who made your raw materials out of nothing.

God, thank You for my creative talents. How should I best apply them in the coming days?

WE DO ORDINARY WORKS

Then I [Nehemiah] told them of the hand of my God which was good upon me; as also the king's words that he had spoken unto me. And they said, Let us rise up and build. So they strengthened their hands for this good work.
NEHEMIAH 2:18 KJV

When we consider work, we mostly think of the hours we spend at our job. For many of us, it's hard to imagine much of that counting for eternity. But any work that's done well, for God's glory, reflects His image. And He honors that.

Think about it: God Himself worked for six days, rested the seventh, and ever since "is always at his work to this very day" (John 5:17).

Recall, too, that Jesus was a tradesman from at least the age of twelve until age thirty (Matthew 13:55, Mark 6:3, and Luke 3:23). Traditionally, Jesus has been called a carpenter, obviously working with wood. Then again, in that time He probably also worked with stone and other materials. He likely performed common labor too, including transporting raw materials and finished goods.

Jesus often talked with and about agricultural workers, builders, day laborers, farmers, fishermen, farmhands, household servants, hired (temporary) shepherds, merchants, physicians, soldiers, tax collectors, vineyard owners, vineyard workers, watchmen, and others.

And the rest of the Bible describes embroiderers, linen workers, metalworkers, stonemasons, tanners, tentmakers, weavers, and many other craftsmen. Doesn't it seem like work is important to God?

Business professor and author Tom Heetderks says these ten important words: "God can use anyone, and He wants to use you." The issue isn't what you do or how exciting (or boring) it is. Instead, it's how you do your work (wholeheartedly) and for whom (God).

God never looks down on certain jobs, including yours. He only cares that your work reflects His work—that it is done well for His glory.

God, I promise to do my best for You, especially when I'm doing ordinary stuff at work.

WE DO GOOD WORKS

Oh that men would praise the LORD for his goodness,
and for his wonderful works to the children of men!
PSALM 107:8 (ALSO 15, 21, 31) KJV

Yes, today's scripture is repeated four times on one page. Other verses in the Psalms in the King James Version also celebrate God's "wonderful works" (40:5, 78:4, and 111:4). And Acts 2:11 (KJV) quotes men from many nations who are listening to the apostles and saying "we do hear them speak in our tongues the wonderful works of God."

Of course, these are only a few of the many Bible verses that describe God's wonderful works from creation (Genesis 1–2) to eternity (Revelation 21–22). In turn, God wants *us*, men made in His image, to do many good works that will count for eternity.

Surprisingly, Jesus rebuked those who told Him about their own "wonderful works" (Matthew 7:22 KJV). The Lord doesn't want us talking a good talk. Instead,

He wants us to steadfastly keep quiet and actively serve as His hands and feet.

Hands and feet don't talk. Instead, the best hands and feet do what God wants done day after day, week after week, month after month, year after year, and decade after decade.

In other words, let your actions do all the talking. Jesus put it this way: "Let your light so shine before men, that they may see your good works, and glorify your Father which is in heaven" (Matthew 5:16 KJV, an idea echoed in 1 Peter 2:12).

Jesus said, "Whosoever shall give to drink unto one of these little ones a cup of cold water only in the name of a disciple, verily I say unto you, he shall in no wise lose his reward" (Matthew 10:42 KJV). In other words, even the little things count for eternity.

Go and do likewise!

God, I don't want to be a mouth. May I be Your hands and feet again today.

WE FEED THE HUNGRY

*"Look at the birds in the sky. They do
not plant seeds. They do not gather grain.
They do not put grain into a building to keep.
Yet your Father in heaven feeds them!"*
MATTHEW 6:26 NLV

When was the last time you fed a bird? If you're eating on a large pier in Seattle or San Francisco or San Diego, where the signs warn, DON'T FEED SEAGULLS!, you certainly might be tempted.

If you're in a neighborhood full of trees, you might set up a feeder so you can enjoy seeing some medium- and small-sized birds up close. If your yard is full of flowers, you may set up a nectar dispenser to attract hummingbirds. If you live near the wilderness or a large park, you may watch eagles, hawks, osprey, and other large-winged predators enjoying small animals or fresh fish.

The reality is that the Lord God, who has created

roughly a hundred billion birds, is the One who feeds them all the time. Imagine that job! Yet to God, it's important. Feeding the birds of the sky is but one illustration of His commitment to provide sustenance to birds, fish, and all other living things.

As men made in God's image, we too have a built-in commitment to provide sustenance (and more) to other creatures—especially to our children, wives, aging parents, and other dependents, as well as the needy in our community. If we can sponsor a needy child overseas, all the better.

We feed others by the sweat of our brow and our tireless commitment to treat others as if they were Jesus, as Matthew 25 instructs us. It's what men who are made in the image of God do.

Lord, thank You for feeding the birds of the air and giving me the task of providing sustenance to my loved ones and those in need. It gives my work even more meaning.

WE PROVIDE CLEAN WATER

"The King will say to those on his right,
'Come, you who are blessed by my Father;
take your inheritance, the kingdom prepared
for you since the creation of the world. For I was
hungry and you gave me something to eat, I was
thirsty and you gave me something to drink.'"

MATTHEW 25:34-35

More than a third of humanity lacks it, but everybody needs clean water.

Adam and Eve needed fresh water every day (Genesis 2:6, 10). Abraham gave away some of his land with the best water (Genesis 13:10). God provided Hagar and Ishmael with a well of fresh water in their time of greatest need (Genesis 21:19). Isaac and his large household rejoiced over digging a new well full of water (Genesis 26:32-33).

In the wilderness, the Israelite people demanded water (Exodus 15:22-25) and more water (Exodus 17:1-6) and still more water (Numbers 20:2–8). Centuries later, the apostle Paul explained that physical thirst in spiritual terms: "They all drank the same holy drink. They drank from a holy Rock that went along with them. That holy Rock was Christ" (1 Corinthians 10:4 NLV).

Thankfully, the Promised Land had rivers and streams and springs and wells full of good water. Not everyone had equal access, however, to that water. As we see in today's scripture, good and godly men gladly provided fresh water to others. Today, good and godly Christian men can do the same for more than a third of humanity.

How? Through a reputable charity focused on this life-saving substance. Do some online research or see if your church supports a clean-water ministry for the thirsty of our world. You might give money toward the mission or even volunteer to help out. Either way, you'll be reflecting the image of the God who created water and "sends rain on the righteous and the unrighteous" (Matthew 5:45).

Lord of creation, I thank You for the clean water that I regularly enjoy. Guide me into ways of helping people around the world to enjoy that blessing as well.

WE CLOTHE THE POOR

*"For I was hungry and you gave Me food to eat.
I was thirsty and you gave Me water to drink.
I was a stranger and you gave Me a room. I had
no clothes and you gave Me clothes to wear."*
<small>MATTHEW 25:35–36 NLV</small>

We reflect the image of Jesus Christ (and His earliest followers) when we provide much-needed clothing for the poor, especially the homeless. What's more, when we do so, we clothe Jesus Christ Himself. At least that's what Jesus says in the scripture above.

Such thoughts motivated Mother Teresa (1910–97), the famed missionary to Calcutta, India. She is quoted as saying, "There is always the danger that we may just do the work for the sake of the work. This is where the respect and the love and the devotion come in—that we do it to God, to Christ, and that's why we try to do it as beautifully as possible."

Mother Teresa also said, "We think sometimes that

poverty is only being hungry, naked and homeless. The poverty of being unwanted, unloved and uncared for is the greatest poverty."

So, when we clothe the poor, we do so beautifully, with great love and care. We clothe the person inside and out. We ask for, learn, and use his or her name. We ask for his or her story. We listen to that story patiently, no matter how long it takes.

Furthermore, we recognize but do not judge evidence of poverty or poor choices, emotional or mental illness, or alcoholism or drug abuse.

We provide coats, jackets, shirts, skirts, pants, underwear, socks, and shoes. In wintery times, we provide hats, scarves, raincoats, overcoats, leather gloves, wool socks, and boots. In warm seasons, we provide short sleeve shirts, blouses, shorts, dresses, sandals, and sunscreen lotion. We do these things with love, not judgment.

We bless as God does, when He "causes his sun to rise on the evil and the good, and sends rain on the righteous and the unrighteous" (Matthew 5:45).

God, I see now that donating clothing or money every once in a while isn't enough. May I be Your loving hands and feet within the next day by helping to cloth someone in need.

WE INFLUENCE OUR WORLD

*Live clean, innocent lives as children of
God, shining like bright lights in a world
full of crooked and perverse people.*
PHILIPPIANS 2:15 NLT

In biblical terms, "the world" covers the earth, but the earth isn't always identical to the "world." The phrase "the world" can indicate the social, governmental, and economic structures led by Satan. This system overshadows the affairs of men and women, youth and children who aren't yet actively following Jesus Christ.

Men seeking God and following His Word on earth are "in the world" but aren't part of that system. Instead, they shine as lights within that dark, evil system. After His resurrection, Jesus commanded His followers to tell "people about me everywhere—in Jerusalem, throughout Judea, in Samaria, and to the ends of the earth" (Acts 1:8 NLT).

In turn, Peter and John declared about Jesus,

"There is salvation in no one else! God has given no other name under heaven by which we must be saved" (Acts 4:12 NLT). Therefore, call on the name of the Lord and be saved (Romans 10:13).

Is this good news only for "nice" people? Just the opposite, according to the apostle Paul. " 'Christ Jesus came into the world to save sinners'—and I am the worst of them all" (1 Timothy 1:15 NLT).

Why should Christian men, made in God's image, reject the world system and all it stands for? "Don't you realize that friendship with the world makes you an enemy of God?" (James 4:4 NLT). Therefore, "Do not love this world nor the things it offers you" (1 John 2:15 NLT).

Never forget: "the Spirit who lives in you is greater than the spirit who lives in the world" (1 John 4:4 NLT).

God, I thank You for pouring Your Holy Spirit into me so I have the power to live a clean, innocent life as Your son in this dark world. Please continue remaking me to be more clean and innocent.

WE DELIGHT IN GOD'S FAMILY

*We were especially delighted to see how
happy Titus was, because his spirit has
been refreshed by all of you.*
2 CORINTHIANS 7:13

The Trinity delights in Jesus Christ's church around the world and down through the ages. As men made in God's image, so should we.

God's joy in His people is real in spite of the church's faults. After all, the Father, the Son, and the Holy Spirit can see the church as a beautiful bride who is being adorned for the wedding feast in glory. What a day of rejoicing that will be!

For now, God wants *us* to rejoice in our own local church, attend it regularly, plant our roots deeply into it, thank Him for it, and make it our love and joy. If we do, we set the stage for our children to delight in God's family too.

Bible writers model this for us in specific, practical ways.

First, attend church with joy and anticipation: "not giving up meeting together, as some are in the habit of doing, but encouraging one another—and all the more as you see the Day approaching" (Hebrews 10:25).

Second, speak well of your church: "I take great pride in you. I am greatly encouraged [and] . . .my joy knows no bounds" (2 Corinthians 7:4).

Third, pray for your church: "In all my prayers for all of you, I always pray with joy" (Philippians 1:4).

Fourth, praise your friends within your church: "My brothers and sisters, you whom I love and long for, my joy and crown, stand firm in the Lord in this way, dear friends!" (Philippians 4:1).

Fifth, look forward to eternity: "For what is our hope, our joy, or the crown in which we will glory in the presence of our Lord Jesus when he comes? Is it not you? Indeed, you are our glory and joy" (1 Thessalonians 2:19–20).

God, many things in this world fight for my attention—may I delight in my local church this Sunday.

WE DELIGHT IN GOD'S WORD

I delight in your decrees; I will not neglect your word.
PSALM 119:16

One part of being made in God's image is our ability to communicate. God created words (and His Word) in order to pass along truths human beings need to survive and flourish. As such, we as Christian men should delight in the scriptures.

Today's key verse is from Psalm 119, with 176 verses the longest chapter in the Bible. All the way through, the psalmist repeatedly affirms his delight in God's Word:

- Psalm 119:24: "Your statutes are my delight; they are my counselors."
- Psalm 119:35: "Direct me in the path of your commands, for there I find delight."
- Psalm 119:47: "I delight in your commands because I love them."
- Psalm 119:111 (NLT): "Your laws are my treasure; they are my heart's delight."

- Psalm 119:174: "I long for your salvation, LORD, and your law gives me delight."

What's more, the psalmist's delight in scripture continues no matter what, even amidst difficult people and perilous situations.

- Psalm 119:70: "Their hearts are callous and unfeeling, but I delight in your law."
- Psalm 119:77: "Let your compassion come to me that I may live, for your law is my delight."
- Psalm 119:92: "If your law had not been my delight, I would have perished in my affliction."
- Psalm 119:143: "Trouble and distress have come upon me, but your commands give me delight."

May *we* never let anything rob us of delighting in God's Word.

God, I'm reading this because I do delight in Your Word. May I share that joy with someone else within the next day.

WE BEAR MUCH FRUIT

"Yes, I [Jesus] am the vine; you are the branches. Those who remain in me, and I in them, will produce much fruit. For apart from me you can do nothing . . . . When you produce much fruit, you are my true disciples. This brings great glory to my Father."

JOHN 15:5, 8 NLT

Because we are made in God's image, we can bear the fruit of His Spirit. When we act righteously and don't give up (Galatians 6:9), we reap a "harvest of righteousness" (2 Corinthians 9:10, Hebrews 12:11, and James 3:18).

In this same vein, the apostle Paul urges God's believers to "live a life worthy of the Lord and please him in every way: bearing fruit in every good work, growing in the knowledge of God, being strengthened with all power according to his glorious might so that you may have *great endurance and patience*" (Colossians 1:10–11, emphasis added).

The key to stick-to-it-ness? We need to keep receiving a small part of God's infinite and eternal might, power, and strength. With God, nothing is impossible. Without God, nothing is possible. Jesus says as much in today's scripture: "Apart from me you can do nothing."

The key question to ask ourselves: Will this count for eternity?

If the answer is no, then why are we doing it? Maybe just because it needs to be done. If so, that's valid, but don't let these tasks bog you down. If the answer is yes, then definitely keep doing it. The more fruit we bear for eternity, the better. Jesus adds to today's key scripture by saying, "I chose you and appointed you so that you might go and bear fruit—*fruit that will last*" (John 15:16, emphasis added).

The keys: (1) Act righteously. (2) Continue asking for God's power to flow through you. (3) Remember that God's power always produces good fruit in time. (4) Keep at it!

God, You know I've quit too many times to count. Change me into a man who keeps being strengthened by You, and who keeps bearing fruit that counts for eternity. Amen.

WE ENJOY GOD'S PURITY

So rejoice in the LORD and be glad, all you who obey him! Shout for joy, all you whose hearts are pure!
PSALM 32:11 NLT

Some shudder at the thought of God's absolute blamelessness, brightness, glory, holiness, integrity, perfection, righteousness, sincerity, and sinlessness.

Others shudder at their own dirty hands and feet and lack of a clean heart. Thankfully, this latter group must only look to heaven for confession and repentance, forgiveness and cleansing, salvation and purity of heart.

Once God gives us a pure heart, we have every reason to celebrate before Him and others. We see this in the scripture above ("all you" appears twice). We also see this in other joy-filled verses from the psalms:

Psalm 33:1 (NLV) tells us: "Sing for joy in the Lord, you who are right with Him. It is right for the pure in heart to praise Him."

Psalm 73:1 says, "Surely God is good to...those who are pure in heart." (Indeed!)

Psalm 97:11 (NLV) says: "Light is spread like seed for those who are right and good, and joy for the pure in heart."

The reality is, we enjoy God's purity best when we celebrate it with others. It brings out the purest, deepest love for our brethren.

As 1 Peter 1:22 (KJV) says, "Seeing ye have purified your souls in obeying the truth through the Spirit unto unfeigned love of the brethren, see that ye love one another with a pure heart fervently."

A man has a pure heart of gold—a heart that reflects God's own—when he can sincerely say, "I was reading my men's devotional book. It encouraged me to tell a Christian brother that I love him. I picked you. I hope that's okay!"

God, I thank You for Your purity and love. You've brought a specific friend to mind. I love him and will tell him before day's end.

WE ENJOY WORSHIP AND PRAISE

With my mouth I will greatly extol the LORD; in the great throng of worshipers I will praise him.
PSALM 109:30

The Bible spends hundreds of pages talking about worship and praise. It is the good and appropriate response of men made in God's image: we bless Him, He blesses us back, and we experience deeper love for those around us. It's a win for everyone!

First and foremost, the Bible says that we exalt, glorify, honor, magnify, praise, and worship the Lord God alone (see Genesis 4:26, Exodus 20:3, Deuteronomy 10:20, Deuteronomy 13:4, Joshua 24:14, 2 Kings 17:36, Isaiah 26:13, Matthew 4:10, and Revelation 15:4).

Conversely, scripture couldn't be more obvious in saying that our praise should never go to anyone or anything else, no matter how awe-inspiring. Wicked king Manasseh learned this the hardest way (2 Chronicles 33:11–13; see also Exodus 20:3–5, Leviticus 26:1,

Jeremiah 25:6, 1 Corinthians 5:11, 6:9-10 and 10:14, Acts 17:16, Romans 1:23, Ephesians 5:5, Colossians 3:5, 1 Peter 4:3, and Revelation 21:27).

Praise includes a growing reverence for who God truly is, which in turn imparts wisdom to us (see Deuteronomy 5:29 and 10:12-20, Job 28:28, Psalm 111:10 and 112:1, Proverbs 1:7, 3:7, 9:10 and 15:33, Ecclesiastes 12:13, and Philippians 2:12).

Praise sometimes includes an especially intense desire for the Lord. Two classic examples are Psalm 42:1-4 and 63:1-8.

Then again, praising God isn't always expressive. It can also involve quietness and waiting (see Psalm 37:7 and 46:10, Isaiah 26:3, 30:15 and 40:31, Lamentations 3:24, and Zephaniah 3:17).

What form of praising God appeals most to you right now?

God, I want to praise You today.
Remind me to do so through the
morning, afternoon, and evening.
For You are worthy.

WE FOLLOW GOD'S WORD

*I used to wander off until you disciplined
me; but now I closely follow your word.*
PSALM 119:67 NLT

Adam, Noah, Abraham, Isaac, Jacob, Joseph. None
of these great men of God had a page of scripture—
God spoke directly to them. They heard His words
loud and clear, and there was no mistaking what God
said and meant. Still, half of them had a hard time
following God's orders. Yes, Adam messed up royally,
but we all can be glad Noah obeyed for 120 years
straight.

We have all been made in God's image, but the
sin that permeates our world keeps us from reflecting that image perfectly. Most men are more like
the psalmist quoted above: it takes a series of ter-
rible consequences to get us to stop wandering and
choose to follow God's Word. Unless we're directly
disobeying God in high-handed ways, He doesn't

typically clobber us. Real life does the job for Him.

Instead, God disciplines us in love (Proverbs 3:11-12, Hebrews 12:5-6, and Revelation 3:19) for our own good (Deuteronomy 8:5, Psalm 94:12, Isaiah 38:16, and Hebrews 12:7-11) in order for us to cultivate self-discipline (2 Timothy 1:7 and Titus 1:8).

Thankfully, God happily, purposefully, and abundantly blesses us when we follow Him and His Word in our work, our marriages, our families, our friendships, our local churches, our hobbies, and other spheres of our lives.

Out of sheer self-interest, we should follow God's Word day in and day out. It's truly in our best interests. If only we honestly believed that.

The blessed man blesses others. In what ways can your obedience lead to blessing someone else today? What has God taught you during your time with Him this morning that can help someone else?

God, I want to be a man who is passionate about following the precepts in Your Word. I ask that Your Holy Spirit lead and direct my every step today. And that He would give me an opportunity to bless others.

WE FOLLOW WISDOM

*"But wisdom is shown to be right
by the lives of those who follow it."*
LUKE 7:35 NLT

It's always good to be reminded that to be born is to be tagged "Made by God in His Image." True, sin mars that image, but God's Son and Holy Spirit remake us. This is especially the case when it comes to wisdom.

A baby cannot think rationally. He can only feel. A child who receives worldly information from un-biblical or anti-biblical sources alone can't understand or follow God's infinite, eternal wisdom.

How wise is God? He knows everything. . .and much, much more.

Remember phone books? They contained a million facts but none that could change your life. By themselves, facts are stupid.

God not only has all knowledge but also all discernment, all insight, all understanding, all wisdom, and all in far-above-our-heads ways. The Lord put it like this: "For my thoughts are not your thoughts, neither are your ways my ways. . . . As the heavens are higher than the earth, so are my ways higher than your ways and my thoughts than your thoughts" (Isaiah 55:8–9).

In other words, "God alone knows" is multiplied by infinity and eternity.

None of us knows 0.000001 percent of everything that's true and right and important and life-changing. So why in the world are we ever tempted to think we know better than God? We know better than Him how to run our lives? Not a chance.

God's wisdom permeates your life. Humbly acknowledge His higher, heavenly wisdom and ways today. Seek out opportunities to tell someone, "In the Bible, I learned. . ."

God, through Your Word and godly men, I have learned what's true, important, life-changing, and eternally valuable. Today I'll tell someone, "In the Bible I learned. . .". My smile will be aimed at You!

WE GIVE THANKS

We always pray and give thanks to God for you.
COLOSSIANS 1:3 NLV

Chapter for chapter, no other book of the Bible says "thank," "thanks," and "thankful" more than Paul's letter to the Colossian believers. It even beats out Psalms by a mile. So what can we learn from Colossians?

Today's key verse says "we give thanks to God." We see this again in the next two verses. Colossians 1:4 (NLV) says: "We give thanks to God for you because we heard of your faith in Christ Jesus. We thank God for your love for all those who belong to Christ." (May both be said of us too.) Colossians 1:5 (NLV) adds: "We thank God for the hope that is being kept for you in heaven. You first heard about this hope through the Good News which is the Word of Truth."

After giving thanks to God, we share our rock-solid hope with others. Colossians 1:12 (NLV) says, "I pray that you will be giving thanks to the Father. He has made it so you could share the good things given to those who belong to Christ who are in the light."

Ultimately, we grow into a life full of thanks. Colossians 2:7 (NLV) states, "Have your roots planted deep in Christ. Grow in Him. Get your strength from Him. Let Him make you strong in the faith as you have been taught. Your life should be full of thanks to Him" or, as 3:16 (NLV) says, your heart should be "full of thanks to God." Finally, Colossians 3:15 and 4:2 say we're to give thanks always, just as today's scripture indicates.

Since God created and provides everything, He doesn't need to say "thank you" to anyone. But the emphasis on thanks in scripture clearly indicates that gratitude is important to Him. As men made in His image, let's give thanks. . .and make God's heart glad.

God, I want to make Your heart glad. Let me begin by giving thanks to You for my family, my employment, my church, my health, my friends, and the many blessings You've provided.

WE ENCOURAGE OTHERS

*Jonathan went to find David and encouraged
him to stay strong in his faith in God.*
1 SAMUEL 23:16 NLT

God encourages His people. In turn, as men made in
His image, we are to encourage other guys. Job encouraged many people. Moses encouraged Joshua. Joshua
encouraged God's people. Gideon encouraged his three
hundred men. Jonathan encouraged David. David encouraged his men. Jehoshaphat encouraged his people
to return to the Lord their God. Hezekiah encouraged
the Levites, his military officers, and his people.

Repentant Manasseh encouraged his people to
return to the Lord their God. Josiah encouraged the
priests. Haggai and Zechariah encouraged the Jewish elders. Jesus told some of those He healed, "Be
encouraged!" And the apostles of Jesus nicknamed
Joseph the Levite from Cyprus, calling him "Son of
Encouragement" (Acts 4:36).

It's no surprise that the words *encourage*, *encouraging*, and *encouraged* appear a dozen more times throughout the book of Acts of the Apostles, and three dozen more times through the epistles by Paul, Peter, John, and the writer of Hebrews. Encouragement was a hallmark of the early church. God encouraged them left and right, and they, in turn, encouraged each other.

God also encourages you. Thank Him, then pass the encouragement along. Ask God to bring someone to mind. Don't just send an email—try to meet face to face. Thank your friend for being a friend. Express appreciation for his example in specific ways. Then send him a scan or copy of this particular devotional.

After encouraging your friend, you'll feel encouraged yourself. That's the way God works.

God, I thank You for encouraging me
by sending mentors and friendships
my way. Now use me to encourage
other men before day's end.

WE FORGIVE OTHERS

*"The LORD, the LORD, the compassionate and
gracious God, slow to anger, abounding in love
and faithfulness, maintaining love to thousands,
and forgiving wickedness, rebellion and sin."*
EXODUS 34:6-7

When did Moses display the utmost courage? Speaking
for the Lord God to Pharaoh? Calling down the worst
of the plagues? Asking the Lord to part the Red Sea?
Receiving the Ten Commandments from the Lord's
own hand?

Actually, right before that last event, Moses asked
the Lord for the impossible: "Now show me your glory"
(Exodus 33:18). The Lord knew what Moses meant and
replied: "You cannot see my face, for no one may see
me and live" (Exodus 33:20). Still, the Lord put Moses
in a cleft in the rock, covered it with His hand, and
passed by proclaiming His name, as we see in today's
scripture.

Of everything the Lord could have said about Himself (and that's a lot!), He chose to focus on His compassion, grace, patience, love, and faithfulness—and therefore His willingness to forgive "wickedness, rebellion and sin." This amazing proclamation reverberates throughout the rest of the Old Testament and unlocks our understanding of Jesus Christ in the Gospels.

If our heavenly Father willingly forgives the worst of sinners (including vicious Naaman the Syrian, exceedingly wicked King Manasseh, and murderous Saul the persecutor), what about us? As men made in God's image, yes, we can and should forgive the worst deeds by our own prodigals and opponents alike.

Forgiving the worst is wretchedly painful. Everything naturally within us screams no. Yet it's what men who are made in God's image always do. . .as our forgiving God provides us the power.

___

Lord, thank You for forgiving all my sins, past, present, and future. You know everything I've done, yet You show compassion, grace, patience, love and faithfulness. May I do the same for others.

WE GUIDE OTHERS

*For this God is our God for ever and ever;
he will be our guide even to the end.*

PSALM 48:14

Throughout the Psalms, God is often described as guiding His people. Besides today's scripture, Psalm 25:5 says, "Guide me in your truth and teach me, for you are God my Savior." Psalm 25:9 indicates that "He guides the humble in what is right and teaches them his way." Psalm 31:3 reads, "Since you are my rock and my fortress, for the sake of your name lead and guide me." Psalm 73:24 promises, "You guide me with your counsel, and afterward you will take me into glory." And there are many other references in Psalms to the way God helps His people to find the right path, to do the right thing, to live the right life.

As men made in His image, we have a responsibility to help others to know, honor, and obey our God. As He has guided us into salvation and spiritual growth—

most likely through the words and example of other Christians—we should do this for the men God brings into our lives.

Don't ever think that you're not qualified or capable of the jobs God gives you. He will always provide the power for the purpose He assigns. As another familiar psalm says, "Where can I go from your Spirit? Where can I flee from your presence? If I go up to the heavens, you are there; if I make my bed in the depths, you are there. If I rise on the wings of the dawn, if I settle on the far side of the sea, even there your hand will guide me, your right hand will hold me fast" (Psalm 139:7-10).

To have a successful journey through a dangerous land, you need a guide. For you, God Himself has been that guide, and He has provided human guides as well. Now work with Him to be a guide for others.

Father in heaven, thank You for guiding me through this dark and perilous world. Use me now to guide others into the safety of Your wings.

WE KEEP OUR PROMISES

*So I will sing thanks to Your name forever
and keep my promises day by day.*
PSALM 61:8 NLV

Scripture contains relatively few promises by men to God, and frankly half of those are lame or stupid. Instead, what we mostly find in the Bible are hundreds of promises made by God to others. Specifically, we find four types of promises God makes by His grace. Each type or group of promises is relational in nature. Ultimately, they all have to do with bringing people into God's family.

The first type are the promises God made over thousands of years, from Genesis 3 to Malachi 4 about and to the Messiah, Jesus Christ, our Lord and Savior. In essence, these promises provide the divine purpose or rationale for the three other types of promises God has made.

The second type are the promises God made over

the course of two thousand years about and to the Israelites in both the Old and New Testaments, from Genesis 12 to Revelation 21–22.

The third type are the promises God made from Genesis 12 to Revelation 21–22 about and to the Gentiles, inviting them to be His people as well.

The fourth type are the promises God made over three generations, from Matthew 5 to Revelation 21–22 to the church, which includes all Christians down through the ages since Pentecost (Acts 2).

Amazingly, the Bible makes a point in describing believers in each group as adopted "children of the promise" (Romans 9:8), inheritors and heirs (Galatians 4:28, Hebrews 6:12 and 6:17).

To honor the heavenly Father, in whose image they're made, Christian men keep their word no matter how inconvenient or costly (Psalm 15:4). They also repair broken promises.

God, give me the strength to keep
any promises I make. And when I fail,
please help me to make repairs.

WE ALWAYS PERSEVERE, PART 1

For if you possess these qualities in increasing measure, they will keep you from being ineffective and unproductive in your knowledge of our Lord Jesus Christ. . . . For if you do these things, you will never stumble, and you will receive a rich welcome into the eternal kingdom of our Lord and Savior Jesus Christ.

2 PETER 1:8, 10–11

The more unjustified, brutal pain, suffering, grief, and loss we experience, the easier it gets. Easier, that is, for us to justify bitterness, white lies, "little" sins, self-pride, financial cheating, power grabbing, sexual fantasies, and the lot.

This doesn't mean that the older we get, the easier it is to *not* sin. Just the opposite. Instead, it gets easier to justify what we want, do what we want, and see if we can get away with or dodge any immediate repercussions. If so, we start justifying even more of what we want to do.

What a disaster.

The question is: Will you keep the faith, do great things for God even in old age, and have a God-honoring legacy for generations to come? Think of the perseverance of Jesus Himself, the very God in whose image you're made, who "for the joy set before him. . .endured the cross, scorning its shame, and sat down at the right hand of the throne of God" (Hebrews 12:2).

The Bible offers other real-life stories of numerous heroes (and villains) of the faith. The Holy Spirit recorded these blunt accounts to inspire us to turn from pride and self-indulgence and back to God on our knees. He recorded them to move us to repent, ask for forgiveness, and make a serious commitment.

That commitment—to God and close Christian friends—might be to review, memorize, study, and meditate on today's scripture. This could be the most important turning point in your life. Make it count!

God, I don't want disaster. Instead,
I want to finish well. Therefore, I'm making
a commitment to live out today's scripture.
Please help me follow You to the very end.

WE ALWAYS PERSEVERE, PART 2

"But the seed on good soil stands for those with a noble and good heart, who hear the word, retain it, and by persevering produce a crop."

LUKE 8:15

At what point does our heavenly Father say, "That's it! There's no hope for you now. Until the day you die, you're toast"? Thankfully, never!

Then again, at what point do *we* say to God, "That's it! I'm tired of being 'Made by God In His Image.' From now on, I'm going to do my own thing"? Yes, we're all tempted. . .but never, never, never give up or give in. Instead, aspire to be the kind of man Jesus talks about in today's scripture. Aspire to read God's Word daily with a good heart and take every noble action to apply it that very day.

The nineteenth-century British theologian B. F. Westcott said, "Silently and imperceptibly as we work or sleep, we grow strong or we grow weak; and at last some crisis shows us what we have become." Bishop Westcott added that these great occasions "do not make heroes or cowards; they simply reveal them."

So what kind of man are you becoming? Are you developing backbone, boldness, determination, durability, faithfulness, fortitude, grit, guts, mettle, moxie, patience, and persistence? Are you becoming a man of resilience, resolution, stamina, staying power, steadfastness, straightforwardness, stick-to-it-iveness, tenacity, and toughness?

Is God teaching you the meaning of adversity, bravery, conviction, discipline, endurance, fearlessness, gratitude, hardship, insult, joy, keeping the faith, and listening to the Lord?

In this world, we will have trouble—that's a promise from Jesus Himself (John 16:33). But here's another: "the one who stands firm to the end will be saved" (Mark 13:13).

God, I'm committed to finishing well for Your glory, honor, and praise. Yet You know my heart's struggle with so many sins. Transform me into a man who perseveres through my sinful nature into a man who is brave, disciplined, fearless, and motivated.

WE HONOR GOD'S WORD

*"Now that you know these things,
you will be blessed if you do them."*
JOHN 13:17

If you honor God's Word, God will honor and bless you. Jesus says as much above. Scripture itself says that God prospers those who delight in His Word, take it to heart, and apply it in every area of life. How do we know that? Here are a handful of ways from the first half of the Bible.

In Joshua 1:7–9, God promises we will be prosperous and successful if we study His Word, meditate on it daily, and faithfully obey His commands. What more could we ask?

In Ezra 7:6, we read that Ezra was well-versed in the scriptures and the king "granted him everything he asked, for the hand of the LORD his God was on him." God's hand of blessing was on him, indeed! The same can be our experience today.

In Psalm 1:1–3, God promises that anyone who delights in obeying His Word and meditates on it daily will prosper in whatever he does. Why would God repeat such an extravagant promise? Because God wants us to take Him at His Word!

In Psalm 19:7–14, David says God's Word revives our souls, makes us wise, brings us joy, and gives us insight into life if we desire it, delight in it, listen to it, and obey it.

In Psalm 119:97–104, the psalmist says he loves God's Word, which makes him wiser than his enemies, his teachers, and his elders, for he desires scripture, meditates on it "all day long," and always obeys it.

Having been made in God's image—and remade by faith in His Son, Jesus Christ—we honor the Word He's given us. How can you exalt the scripture today?

God, yes, I do want to honor and obey Your Word day by day. Please bless me as I do what You say.

WE HONOR WOMEN

The Lord gives the Word. And the women
who tell the good news are many.
Psalm 68:11 NLV

During His public ministry, Jesus did something revolutionary. It was something the Greeks, Romans, and others never considered.

He elevated the status of women back to the Lord's original intention when He made and blessed Adam and Eve. After all, "He created them male and female and blessed them. And he named them 'Mankind' when they were created" (Genesis 5:2; see also Genesis 1:27–28 and Genesis 2:22–23).

It's moving how Jesus respected, honored, and blessed these women (and many others):

- His earthly mother, Mary, who quietly pondered the stories of Christmas, expressed pride over His actions at the wedding in Cana, fretted about her Son's well-being, wept at His execution, and joined the other believers for Pentecost (Matthew 2:11-14, Matthew 2:19-21, Luke 1:48, Luke 2:15-38, John 2:1-12, John 19:25-27, and Acts 1-2).

- The Samaritan woman, who shared the good news and many believed that Jesus was the Savior of the world (John 4:1-42).
- The women who traveled with Jesus—not only Mary Magdalene, but also "Joanna the wife of Chuza, the manager of Herod's household; Susanna; and many others. These women were helping to support them out of their own means" (Luke 8:3).
- The woman caught in adultery and yet pardoned by Jesus (John 8:1-11).
- The Syrophoenician woman, whose cruelly demon-possessed daughter was healed after Jesus honored her mother in front of her hometown crowd (Matthew 15:21-25 and Mark 7:24-30).

No Christian man follows Jesus wholeheartedly who doesn't consistently honor women. Not just godly women, but not-yet-Christian women as well.

God, Jesus didn't treat women the way I do. Too often, I don't see them as the faithful servants that they are. I repent. Please forgive me.

WE HONOR WIVES

Her husband praises her: "There are many virtuous and capable women in the world, but you surpass them all!" Charm is deceptive, and beauty does not last; but a woman who fears the LORD will be greatly praised. Reward her for all she has done. Let her deeds publicly declare her praise.

PROVERBS 31:28–31 NLT

Only the Lord Himself knows how many articles and sermons, books and seminars have extolled the virtues of the Wonder Woman described in Proverbs 31:10–31. The only problem is that they have usually forgotten to mention the other main character—the Good Husband.

This passage is a four-fold challenge to godly men, made in the Lord's image:

1. *Cherish*: The Good Husband recognizes the true value of his wife as a person (31:10). He sees her as God's priceless, one-of-a-kind masterpiece. He is quick to say. "She is

worth far more than rubies."

2. *Support*: The Good Husband believes in the potential of his wife (31:11). He doesn't put her in a box called "home" only to let her lie there dormant. Instead, he allows her to be productive and fulfilled both in and out of the home (31:16 and 31:20).

3. *Listen*: The Good Husband realizes the importance of listening to (and learning from) the wisdom of his wife (31:26). He is spared from many rash and foolish actions by respecting that "wisdom, and faithful instruction is on her tongue."

4. *Praise*: The Good Husband praises the virtues and accomplishments of his wife (31:29). He doesn't flatter her but praises his wife for her fear of God (31:30) and her successful endeavors (31:31). He lets others know that his wife is a treasure beyond compare!

For the unmarried, this passage is a challenge to *pursue* a woman of godly character, one you can treat as a treasure.

Lord God, I thank You for creating wives. Help me to reflect Your love for them by honoring my own and/ or those married women You've placed in my circles.

WE HONOR MARRIAGE

Marriage should be honored by all, and the marriage bed kept pure, for God will judge the adulterer and all the sexually immoral.

HEBREWS 13:4

Creation and marriage go hand in hand in the Bible.

The Bible begins with creation and then the marriage of the first man and woman. Creation is perfect and Adam and Eve were perfect, sinless, and pure. So pure that they were naked and unashamed.

The Bible ends with the marriage feast of the Lamb and then the creation of the new heavens and earth. Jesus Christ is perfect, sinless, and pure. So is His Bride, the church. How? Revelation 19:7–8 says, "his bride has made herself ready. Fine linen, bright and clean, was given her to wear."

Then verse 8 goes on to tell us, "Fine linen stands for the righteous acts of God's holy people." This is possible only because we're made in God's image, we have God's Holy Spirit poured into us, and we *want* to do what pleases our Lord and Savior.

In Ephesians 5:23-27, the apostle Paul explains this further: "Christ is the head of the church, his body, of which he is the Savior. Now as the church submits to Christ, so also wives should submit to their husbands in everything. Husbands, love your wives, just as Christ loved the church and gave himself up for her to make her holy, cleansing her by the washing with water through the word, and to present her to himself as a radiant church, without stain or wrinkle or any other blemish, but holy and blameless."

In verse 32, Paul adds that marriage "is a profound mystery—but I am talking about Christ and the church." This is true whether we're single, married, separated, divorced, or widowed. We are the Bride of Christ, made in His image for Him.

God, You know my situation. More importantly, You know how history's grand story ends. Keep me pure and blameless as I await Your return.

WE HONOR OUR PARENTS

"Honor your father and mother." This is the first commandment with a promise: If you honor your father and mother, "things will go well for you, and you will have a long life on the earth."
<small>EPHESIANS 6:2–3 NLT</small>

Most Western cultures lost their hold on this command a few generations ago. For five billion other people, honoring one's parents is deeply embedded in their cultures. Most not-yet-Christians in Asia, Africa, and other regions therefore gladly affirm the Fifth Commandment. The honor they show to their parents and ancestors, they believe, will come back to them as honor shown by their children and posterity.

What about Christian men today? How can we honor our parents (if they are still alive) or our parents' memories (if they are deceased)? And what about if they weren't good parents who are seemingly undeserving of honor?

The first question is a little easier to answer. We can honor them in a myriad of ways—by listening to or passing on their stories, by asking them for advice or by sharing their wisdom with younger generations, by taking care of them when they are ill or by taking the time to honor their memory, and more.

The second question is a difficult one, but we know that the Christian is called to a life of forgiveness. And when we do so, we are bound to not bring up past offenses. (Of course, if someone has committed a crime against us, this doesn't let them off the hook in a legal sense.) But as far as we are concerned, we honor God by forgiving our parents in our heart. This reflects the image of our forgiving God.

God, how do You want me to honor my parents today? A phone call? A visit? By becoming their caregiver? By forgiving them? Or in some other fashion?

WE HONOR SENIOR CITIZENS

"Stand up in the presence of the aged, show respect for the elderly and revere your God. I am the LORD."
LEVITICUS 19:32

During His public ministry here on earth, Jesus showed love and respect to people of all ages. Oh, He even loved and respected the hypocritical religious leaders—enough to rebuke them vigorously in hopes of leading them to repentance. In turn, people of all ages loved and respected Jesus.

Though the Bible contains many stories of babies (including Jesus Himself), it's also full of old-timers. The elderly men include Adam, Enoch, Noah, Job, Abraham, Isaac, Jacob, Joseph, Amram and his two sons Moses and Aaron, Joshua, Jehoiada, Isaiah, Daniel, Simeon, and John.

The least-known name in that list, Jehoiada, lived to be 130 years old (2 Chronicles 24:15). He's the last Old Testament hero of faith to live well past a century.

The great things he did for God are summarized in 2 Kings 11–12 and 2 Chronicles 22:11–24. Those great accomplishments were overthrowing Judah's murderous queen, establishing a new monarch, leading a national revival, and restoring the temple to its former glory.

Unlike every other Old Testament priest, Jehoiada received an exceptional honor at his death. We read about this in 2 Chronicles 24:16 (NLT): "He was buried among the kings in the City of David, because he had done so much good in Israel for God and his Temple."

What exceptional honors can we give to the godliest old men we know before they die, and before serious mental diminishment sets in? Sometimes, the greatest honor is listening to, recording, and preserving their life stories.

For all the rest, at the command of the God in whose image we're made, let's at least stand and show respect.

God, help me to honor the senior citizens in my life the way they deserve.

WE LOVE GOD'S CHURCH

May the Lord make your love increase and overflow for each other and for everyone else, just as ours does for you.
1 Thessalonians 3:12

God couldn't love the church more. In turn, God wants Christian men, who are made in His image, to do the same.

Why is the church so important to God? Because it is the "body" of His Son, Jesus Christ, who is its "head" (Ephesians 5:23, Colossians 1:18). The apostle Paul explained Jesus' body in detail in 1 Corinthians 12:12–27:

Just as a body, though one, has many parts, but all its many parts form one body, so it is with Christ. For we were all baptized by one Spirit so as to form one body—whether Jews or Gentiles, slave or free—and we were all given the one Spirit to drink. Even so the body is not made up of one part but of many. Now if the foot should say, "Because I am not a hand, I do not belong

*to the body," it would not for that reason stop
being part of the body. And if the ear should
say, "Because I am not an eye, I do not belong
to the body," it would not for that reason stop
being part of the body. . . . The eye cannot say
to the hand, "I don't need you!" And the head
cannot say to the feet, "I don't need you!" On
the contrary, those parts of the body that seem
to be weaker are indispensable, and the parts
that we think are less honorable we treat
with special honor. . . . God has put the body
together, giving greater honor to the parts that
lacked it, so that there should be no division in the
body, but that its parts should have equal concern
for each other. If one part suffers, every part
suffers with it; if one part is honored, every part
rejoices with it. Now you are the body of Christ,
and each one of you is a part of it.*

The church—those folks in your local congregation
and every true believer everywhere—is the actual body
of Christ in this world. Love it like God does!

---

*God, thank You for calling me to love my local
church more deeply. Show me ways that I can love
and support my church, starting right now.*

WE LOVE OUR FAMILY

"But while he was still a long way off, his father saw him and was filled with compassion for him; he ran to his son, threw his arms around him and kissed him."

LUKE 15:20

If you've been blessed with a good family, the idea of loving your parents and siblings is a no-brainer. You remember the times of laughter, teamwork, instruction, and even healthy correction that made you the man you are today. Loving a good family doesn't seem to require that much of God's image in you.

But other men have had to deal with a much tougher upbringing. Some parents are selfish, aloof, even abusive. Some siblings fight over everything. Some families don't seem worth loving.

Either way, God calls His children to love, the way the father in Jesus' parable of the lost son did. You may recognize the young man as the "prodigal" (or wasteful) son, who rudely demanded his inheritance *before* his father died. Amazingly, the father gave the boy what he wanted. . .and even more amazingly, watched longingly for his return from the foolish, degrading life he had chosen. When the young man appeared on the horizon, the father was filled with love and joy and actually ran to embrace and kiss him.

The clear implication of Jesus' story is that God the Father views us like that prodigal son. We act selfishly and wander away from Him. . .but He longs for us to come to our senses (verse 17) and be restored to fellowship.

By loving your own family in good times and bad, you reflect the image of God. He provides and protects, guides and corrects with His family, just as you should for yours. And, by His mighty power, you can.

God, I want Your kind of love
for my family. Help me to love
them unconditionally, the way
You have loved me.

WE LOVE OUR NEIGHBORS

"The second is equally important: 'Love your neighbor as yourself.' No other commandment is greater than these."

MARK 12:31 NLT

When someone asked Jesus which commandment is most important, He replied, "You must love the LORD your God with all your heart, all your soul, all your mind, and all your strength" (Mark 12:30 NLT). Then He continued with today's scripture.

In His comments about loving God, Jesus echoed the words of Deuteronomy 6:5. In His words about loving others as ourselves, Jesus quoted Leviticus 19:18. The supreme priority of these two statements stands out more clearly in Matthew 22:40 where Jesus declares, "All the Law and the Prophets hang on these two commandments."

There is nothing more important in all the scriptures, in terms of what God asks of us, than to love

Him wholeheartedly and to love our neighbors as we love ourselves.

When we embrace God's deep love for *us*, we become better able to trust *His* heart and to love *others* in return. Loving what God loves is the key—and yes, He absolutely loves you. In Jeremiah 31:3, the Lord says, "I have loved you with an everlasting love." It's not just corporate—it's also personal.

This isn't selfish. It's the exact opposite. If learning to embrace God's deep love changes how you treat yourself and ultimately enables you to love others better, then the results are decidedly *unselfish*.

The apostle John told us that "God is love" (1 John 4:8). Men made in His image will reflect that love to their neighbors. (And, just in case there's any question regarding who that includes, see Jesus' parable of the good Samaritan in Luke 10:25-37).

God, I embrace Your deep love for me. Please help me to know each of my neighbors, and give me opportunities to show Your love to them. I thank You now for what You're going to do.

WE LOVE IMMIGRANTS

"You should act toward the stranger who lives among you as you would toward one born among you. Love him as you love yourself."
LEVITICUS 19:34 NLV

The early church found itself embracing thousands of immigrants on day one (Acts 2). The city of Jerusalem was filled with foreign-born Jewish individuals, couples, and families from throughout the eastern Mediterranean region and beyond. Many thousands trusted Jesus Christ for salvation and then stayed on in Jerusalem to learn more about their newfound Christian faith.

Fast-forward two thousand years. For those of us who live in the United States, our own land has millions of immigrants from many scores of nations. Many immigrants want to acclimate to our country. Most are eager to adapt and are grateful for any help people can offer them. It's important to distinguish, however, between sharing our culture and sharing our faith.

This isn't easy because we often don't stop to think about the differences.

The goal of "heavenly citizenship" is vastly more important than gaining citizenship here. Don't let your patriotism (or lack thereof) interfere with forming relationships with immigrants. As you do, remember that what immigrants think about your nation is not nearly as important as what they eventually think about Jesus Christ.

Inviting a person to church can be like inviting him into yet another culture. It's not the most effective first step in evangelizing immigrants. It might even be helpful to wait until a few months *after* he trusts Jesus Christ before inviting him to church.

More than any service you could provide, a new immigrant is most blessed by your kindness and friendship. A loving Christian friend is a powerful witness to the good news of Jesus Christ, and an excellent reflection of the image of the Father.

God, I know that there are probably immigrants nearby. Help me to ask them about their story, listen, and develop a friendship to introduce them to Jesus.

WE LOVE REFUGEES

For the LORD your God is God of gods and Lord of lords, the great God, mighty and awesome, who shows no partiality. . . . He defends the cause of the fatherless and the widow, and loves the foreigner residing among you, giving them food and clothing. And you are to love those who are foreigners, for you yourselves were foreigners.

DEUTERONOMY 10:17–19

God's special heart for refugees shows up throughout the scriptures. He commanded the Israelites to show extraordinary care to aliens, foreigners, and strangers—that is, to those who left their country of origin to live among God's people.

These refugees weren't in a position to enjoy the same rights and resources as they had in their own nation. Still, they were to be cared for just as much as Israel's widows and orphans (Exodus 22:21, 23:9, and today's scripture above).

God reminded the Israelites to remember how it felt to be aliens in Egypt and commanded them to show His compassion and love (Deuteronomy 10:19). They were never to adopt the false religions of the foreigners, but God also warned His people not to mistreat them (Jeremiah 7:5-7).

When befriending refugees, you will want to determine if individuals are more interested in hanging on to their cultural identity or quickly assimilating into your nation. The goal is to introduce them to "heavenly citizenship," but first you must understand their motives and desires. This will help you minister to them more effectively.

Not everyone can sponsor a refugee family, providing money, training, or other services. But every Christian man can have a heart and mind to bless the foreigners and strangers God has brought to your shores. Such compassion reflects His image to our world.

God, even Moses and Jesus were refugees. That says a lot. Make me more sensitive to the stories that refugees share and give me an opportunity to minister to one.

WE COMFORT OTHERS

[God] gives us comfort in all our troubles.
Then we can comfort other people who
have the same troubles. We give the
same kind of comfort God gives us.
2 CORINTHIANS 1:4 NLV

God comforts us. It's one of the dozens of ways He proves His goodness. In turn, He calls us to comfort others. In doing so, we exhibit His image in a beautiful way.

When we go through difficult stretches, it helps to remember that God is using those situations to prepare us to minister to others. That thought may not always be on the top of our mind, but it brings great comfort and a sense of purpose to our grief, losses, struggles, and other trials.

How good that God is our source of comfort and solace, encouragement and strength, joy and peace. Need tangible proof? When someone says they are praying for you.

In turn, be encouraged to pray for others who are going through grief. Write a prayer card reminder so you keep praying for them. Then send a greeting card to express your love and ongoing prayers.

If someone loses a loved one, ask if you can bring a meal, help with clean-up after the memorial service, or take care of their car with a wash or oil change. The more menial, time-consuming, and practical the task, the better. By performing that work for a grieving person, you'll shoulder a burden that he or she won't have to carry.

Mostly, remember that grief isn't a checkbox. It never really goes away. So keep praying and touching base with your friend.

And always, point to the Lord God as the ultimate source of comfort and solace, encouragement and strength, and joy and peace.

God, when You bring hurting people into my life, please use me to comfort them with Your love.

WE STUDY GOD'S WORD

So the people went away to eat and drink at a festive meal, to share gifts of food, and to celebrate with great joy because they had heard God's words and understood them.
NEHEMIAH 8:12 NLT

When a group of Christians finally hear God's words in their mother tongue, and Bible teachers help them understand what that scripture passage says, it produces great joy and celebration. This has already happened in more than thirty-four hundred languages.

What about those of us who speak and read English? It's important to find a Bible translation that speaks to your heart. For many, it's the Shakespearean King James Version. For many others, it's a contemporary English translation. For some, it's a combination of versions to read, study, memorize, and read together. Finding the right translation or combination of translations is also helpful when reading the scripture with not-yet-Christians.

No matter what Bible translation we read, we'll never understand it all. Though we are made in our infinite God's image, we are severely limited copies! So, it's essential to write down questions that arise. Millions of other readers have probably asked the same questions.

You'll find many answers in a study Bible published by a reputable publisher. You'll find other answers by talking with your pastor or another theologically-trained friend of yours. Understand though that we'll probably have to wait until heaven for the answers to our best and toughest questions.

You don't have to be Mr. Answer Man to read the Bible with someone else. Applaud his questions and write them down. Don't try to answer them. Just keep reading. Often, your friend will spot the answer later on that same page. That's always fun!

God, I want to know Your Word better. And I want to share it with people who are not-yet-Christians. Set my heart on fire for Your Word.

WE PRAY EARNESTLY

And being in anguish, [Jesus] prayed
more earnestly, and his sweat was like
drops of blood falling to the ground.
LUKE 22:44

Men, who are made in God's image, are called to pray.
As a man, Jesus Himself set that example.

But there are many other biblical men who prayed,
earnestly:

Like Elijah, we know that God will meet our needs
even in the most desperate of circumstances (1 Kings
17–19).

Like Jehoshaphat, we face trials and danger with
songs of praise for God's faithful love (2 Chronicles 20).

Like Manasseh, we realize it's not too late to turn
back to God, repent, and ask for His forgiveness, no
matter how horrible our past (2 Chronicles 33:10–13).

Like Ezra, the great Bible teacher, we pray to God
for safety and protection (Ezra 8:21–23).

Like David, who wrote half of the Psalms, we tell God what's on our heart in any and every circumstance.

Like David's friend Asaph, we turn to God in prayer when something shakes our faith (Psalm 73).

Like Daniel, we cry out to God in crisis situations.

Like Paul, we implore God for our own healing, accepting either the yes or no of His response (2 Corinthians 12:7–10).

God made us to communicate with Himself. He speaks to us through creation, His Word, the Spirit, and our conscience. We respond to Him in prayer. Let's be sure to take advantage of this amazing freedom.

Lord Jesus, You pray more earnestly than we could ever imagine. And You want me also to pray earnestly about what really matters. Give me a heart that is filled with desire for earnest prayer.

WE PRAY FOR WIVES

*Husbands, in the same way be considerate
as you live with your wives, and treat them
with respect as the weaker partner and as
heirs with you of the gracious gift of life,
so that nothing will hinder your prayers.*
1 PETER 3:7

Many readers of this devotional will be married men. Some won't be, due to their own youth, bachelorhood, divorce, or widowhood. Wherever you land on the marriage spectrum, it's good to pray for wives—your own, or the wives of friends and relatives.

Reread today's scripture. The last phrase reminds us that God is God and we are not. Nothing can hinder Him. Sin and other things, however, can hinder us and our prayers.

No wonder Hebrews 12:1 says, "Let us throw off everything that hinders and the sin that so easily entangles. And let us run with perseverance the race marked out for us."

Single or married, your prayers can be hindered by careless attitudes, disrespectful thoughts, inconsiderate words, and graceless actions—not just overt sins against God.

The Christian man who recognizes his status as "made in the image of God" loves the Lord and people (Matthew 22:36-40). Yes, it's easy to say, but oh so hard to live out. Yet live it out we must, or our love would be nothing (1 Corinthians 13:1-3).

The married man must love his wife, as Jesus Christ loved the church (Ephesians 5:25). Part of that is praying like Jesus prayed—specifically and sacrificially. But the unmarried man can also help the marriages of those men around him by imploring God's blessing on their wives.

God loves women (He created them specially), marriage (He set up the institution), and the men who pray for both. Do your part, whether for your own wife or others', and thank God for the stability that a good marriage brings to society.

Lord God, I want to see marriages strengthened, because I know that honors You and benefits our world. May it be so!

WE PRAY FOR CHILDREN

Then people brought little children to Jesus for him to place his hands on them and pray for them. But the disciples rebuked them. Jesus said, "Let the little children come to me, and do not hinder them, for the kingdom of heaven belongs to such as these."
MATTHEW 19:13-14

Since we are made in God's image, we as men should love what He loves. And God loves children.

Whether or not you have kids of your own, you probably have nephews and nieces, or even "adopted" ones. There are certainly children in your neighborhood or church.

Whoever your "children" are, do you want to leave their future up to chance, without great anticipation? Instead, why not pray eagerly, earnestly, and fervently for God's rich blessings on and through them—to bless untold thousands?

Let's never pray for a child to be powerful, rich, or

famous. All three of those things will wither like grass on a hot summer day.

Instead, let's thank God for each child by name. And while we might pray about their homework, hobbies, or healing, it's even better to emphasize God's good work within their hearts (Philippians 1:6, 4:6-7, and 1 Timothy 4:12).

We can pray over college acceptance letters, scholarships, and future spouses, but let's especially ask God to help them live vibrantly for Him (Acts 2:42), to readily identify as His adopted children (1 John 3:1).

Finally, let's pray that all the kids in our life grow up to be courageous, winsome, wise, godly, and righteous young people who love God wholeheartedly and others as themselves (Matthew 22:37-40, Mark 12:29-31, and Luke 10:27).

Few things will make a greater impact on our society and world than a generation of committed, godly young people. Why not offer up a prayer for them now?

God, I don't want to hinder children from coming to You. I want to do the exact opposite, especially through my prayers for the children You've placed in my life.

WE PRAY FOR GOD'S CHURCH

*Pray in the Spirit at all times and on every
occasion. Stay alert and be persistent in
your prayers for all believers everywhere.*
EPHESIANS 6:18 NLT

It's awe-inspiring to remember that our heavenly Father always hears the prayers of His beloved Son, Jesus Christ, and the prayers of His dear Holy Spirit. If the Trinity prays without ceasing, it's no wonder God commands us to do the same.

Thankfully, the Holy Spirit gives us the power to pray. It's up to us, however, to actually pray. Begin by asking for the Spirit's power to flow through you. Then listen for His promptings on how best to pray.

This writer felt prompted to use three-by-five-inch index cards to write down his worship of God, his confession of besetting sins, his personal prayer requests, and his intercessions for others. That stack of cards now is a full inch tall and requires a sturdy rubber band. He prays for half of the cards daily. He uses a blue-edged card to mark his place within the second half of the cards.

As you might have guessed, a number of cards remind him how best to pray for his local church. He prays for its leadership board, staff, and key teachers and preachers. He prays for his closest friends at church. He prays for church members who are fighting cancer and have other major health issues. He prays for widows and others who have lost a family member. He prays for young married couples and singles. He prays for missionaries. And he prays for prodigals.

As you listen for the Holy Spirit's promptings, you very well may be led differently. That's okay. The methods don't matter. It's the consistent heart, made in God's image, that does!

God, please help me to pray daily. It doesn't come naturally. So infuse me with Your Spirit's power and promptings. I'm taking time to listen right now.

WE PRAY FOR LEADERS

I urge, then, first of all, that petitions, prayers, intercession and thanksgiving be made for all people—for kings and all those in authority, that we may live peaceful and quiet lives in all godliness and holiness. This is good, and pleases God our Savior, who wants all people to be saved and to come to a knowledge of the truth.

1 TIMOTHY 2:1-4

What does today's scripture tell us? First, a command. Then, two desirable outcomes.

The command requires "petitions, prayers, intercession, and thanksgiving. . .for all people—for kings and all those in authority." Yes, that includes Democrats, Independents, Republicans, and any other people in government. It's up to you whether to focus on leaders in your city, county, state, or nationally. Start small with two or three names. Add more as God leads. Remember to include "thanksgiving" for what God is going to do in and through them.

The first desirable outcome is "that we may live peaceful and quiet lives in all godliness and holiness. This is good, and pleases God." The second outcome of praying for leaders is that some may "be saved and . . .come to a knowledge of the truth."

Will all be saved? No, but that's what God desires. And we as His children, made in His image, should desire it too. Remember, God is "not wanting anyone to perish, but everyone to come to repentance" (2 Peter 3:9).

Lord God, I can see why it's so important to pray for leaders. Help me to do this duty cheerfully.

WE PRAY FOR MISSIONARIES

And pray for me, too. Ask God to give me the right
words so I can boldly explain God's mysterious plan
that the Good News is for Jews and Gentiles alike.
EPHESIANS 6:19 NLT

Today's scripture is more relevant now than ever. The apostle Paul's Gospel message never varied, but his methods and even vocabulary changed to best meet the needs of his audience. Even today, some missionaries have an itinerant ministry taking them from city to city, country to country, and continent to continent. Jon Dunagan, founder of Harvest Ministry, has served on all seven continents, including Antarctica. Most missionaries, however, have a central base of operations from which they minister.

Get to know your church's missionaries and other friends who are serving God overseas, including businesspeople in otherwise closed countries like Iran, North Korea, and Saudi Arabia. The more you know about them and their particular ministries, the better you can pray.

Download their photos and place them where you'll see them regularly. And subscribe to their newsletters which often include specific prayer requests from them.

You know that both Jesus (Hebrews 7:25) and the Holy Spirit (Romans 8:26) are praying for Christians today, including those who serve God in difficult and dangerous places. Let's reflect the image of God in us by praying regularly for missionaries too.

Father in heaven, give me a passion for people's souls, for those I know personally and those I can affect through my support of missionaries. Please protect and provide for them today.

WE PRAY FOR OUR NEIGHBORS

"May the LORD bless you and protect you. May the LORD smile on you and be gracious to you. May the LORD show you his favor and give you his peace."

NUMBERS 6:24–26 NLT

Are you familiar with this threefold blessing from the Old Testament? Originally, it was a blessing that Moses and Aaron spoke over God's people. It's just as applicable today and is wonderful to say aloud as a blessing for yourself, your family, and your neighbors.

The beginning of each line offers the Lord's *blessing*, *smile*, and *favor*. The second half offers the Lord's great *protection*, gracious *provision*, and grace-filled *peace*. What more could we desire, want, or need?

We see this three-fold blessing echoing throughout the rest of the Hebrew scriptures and the New Testament as well. It reflects God's heart for His people, and it should reflect our own heart toward the people around us. Why not memorize and pray these lines often?

Don't just pray by name *for* your neighbors. Also pray *with* them. You can offer this threefold blessing for your neighbors right before a meal together at your house or theirs.

You also can pray this quick blessing with your eyes open while talking with a neighbor. Tell him, "Here is what I pray," and then quote Numbers 6:24–26. It doesn't get much easier than that.

God, some neighbors are distant and hard to know. Please help me to say hello and consciously learn about them and their needs. Please bless them and me!

WE PRAY FOR PRODIGALS

"I tell you, there is rejoicing in the presence of the angels of God over one sinner who repents."

LUKE 15:10

Right after today's scripture, Jesus told the story of the prodigal son (Luke 15:11–24). Let's not make the mistake, however, of thinking there was only one prodigal back in the day.

These days, is there any realistic hope if someone imitates the prodigal son, wanders away from God and the church, and lives it up in sin season after season? If you're thinking no, you'll likely never pray, let alone pray with hope, for your prodigal friends and relatives.

How good that God doesn't give up on the worst of sinners. The more we remember that, the more we'll pray with hope for the prodigals we know and choose to love.

So, who are these wayward prodigals? They actively followed the Lord Jesus, but later walked away to do their own thing. Often, they walk away from the Bible, then the church, and then anything related to Christianity. This doesn't necessarily mean, however, that they hate Jesus. Sometimes they're simply misinformed and skewed in their understanding. This world is only too happy to cause confusion in people's hearts.

If a wayward prodigal wants to come home spiritually and to know the Lord in a whole new way, God gladly welcomes him or her with open arms. We should too.

Of course, prodigals don't come back in a perfect state, no matter how repentant they may be. Give them plenty of time and reflect lots of God's marvelous, amazing mercy and grace along the way.

God, there are so many people who need Your love and grace—some of them people who've already tasted Your goodness. Please use me to bring them back into Your fold.

WE PRAY FOR UNDERDOGS

How great is the goodness you have stored up for those who fear you. You lavish it on those who come to you for protection, blessing them before the watching world.

PSALM 31:19 NLT

Many of us love cheering on underdogs. Even if they still lose in the end, we like to see an athlete or team give it their best shot. What most people hate, however, are *being* the underdog. Who wants to be poor, pushed around, or persecuted? Who wants to be at the bottom of the heap economically and socially?

How is God relevant in such situations? We discover the answer on almost every page of Psalms. Beginning with Psalm 3, and over and over again until Psalm 149, we see how to pray for the protection of those in dire circumstances.

In seven out of every ten psalms, the writer is either crying out to the Lord for physical salvation, thanking God for sparing his life, reminding himself of the differing fates of the righteous and evildoers, or renewing his allegiance to God and His Word in the face of rampant injustice.

Even the prayer of Moses in Psalm 90, the oldest of all the psalms, is a sorrowful plea for deliverance after years of affliction. Of the thirteen psalm titles that refer to some historical situation in David's life, ten speak of David's enemies pursuing him. Two others indicate David had been delivered from the clutches of a particular evildoer. Of all the psalmists, Solomon alone fails to use the vocabulary of the underdog.

Clearly, God recognizes and cares for the underdog. Often, He's recognizing and caring for you. Sometimes, He wants to use you, reflecting His own compassion to the other underdogs of the world. Pray for them, and listen to what God may be telling you to do.

God, I know at least one person right now who needs Your protection now and in the coming days. Grant it to him, Lord. And remind me of his plight often, so I can continue to pray for him.

WE GIVE SACRIFICIALLY

Jesus called His followers to Him. He said, "For sure, I tell you, this poor woman whose husband has died has given more money than all the others. They all gave of that which was more than they needed for their own living. She is poor and yet she gave all she had, even what she needed for her own living."

MARK 12:43–44 NLV

How often do widows come up in the Gospels? Surprisingly, a lot! The most famous widow's story is found at the end of Mark 12.

This particular woman's religious leaders may have cheated her out of her rightful property (Mark 12:38-40). Conversely, Jesus and His disciples gave alms to the poor regularly and routinely. It's what all godly, good-hearted Jewish men did.

Sadly, however, the poor widow of Mark 12 had been neglected by relatives and overlooked by neighbors. All she had left were two mites, small copper coins worth almost nothing. Yet consider what she did: her small donation proved she was wholly dedicated to the Lord her God. Her love, trust, and bravery clearly moved Jesus, who honored her (see also Luke 21:1–4).

In Matthew 6:21, Jesus tells us: "Where your treasure is, there your heart will be also." The apostle Paul unpacks this in 2 Corinthians 8, especially verse 5: Generous giving is the outflow of all men who give themselves "first of all to the Lord."

The Christian is called to live sacrificially because Christ sacrificed so much for us. Take inventory of your heart today. Do you have the same attitude the poor widow had when it comes to giving? Could you do what she did in today's passage—offering the Lord your last two coins?

Sacrificial giving is never dangerous, because God will always provide for the generous man, made in His image.

God, I'm Yours. Give me the attitude of the poor widow in today's passage. I willingly release my time, money, and possessions to You because You've sacrificed so much for me.

WE PROVIDE FOR OTHERS

*Command those who are rich in this present world
not to be arrogant nor to put their hope in wealth,
which is so uncertain, but to put their hope in God,
who richly provides us with everything for our
enjoyment. Command them to do good, to be rich in
good deeds, and to be generous and willing to share.
In this way they will lay up treasure for themselves
as a firm foundation for the coming age, so that
they may take hold of the life that is truly life.*
1 Timothy 6:17–19

Here's a crazy idea: Drop by your bank and withdraw a
hundred-dollar bill. Hide it in your wallet and tell God
you're ready "to be generous and willing to share." Ask
Him to show you good opportunities to do just that.

Yes, a hundred dollars is a big deal, but that's
where "crazy," "hope in God," "treasures in heaven,"
and "fun" all come together. "I don't have a hundred
dollars to spare!" is exactly the point. None of us can

afford to give away hundred-dollar bills. We're trusting God to supply everything we need, including more hundred-dollar bills.

Keep this hush-hush. It's just between you and God ...and your wife and older children if applicable. Don't say a word about the money to anyone else. If you see someone who needs help, hear him out. Ask three or four well-aimed questions. Then be quiet and listen to what the Holy Spirit nudges you to do.

Ideally, you'll also have a five-dollar bill and a twenty on you. Once the Spirit says which one to give, open your wallet, take it out quickly, close your wallet, smile, and give. Then trust God. After all, it's His money.

He gives to you. As a man made in His image, you give back to Him—by giving to others.

God, make me sensitive to Your leading
as I'm listening to others in need. Then
help me to be generous in response!

WE PURSUE JUSTICE

*When justice is done, it brings joy to
the righteous but terror to evildoers.*
PROVERBS 21:15

Until the end of days, this world will keep mocking God's justice. No matter who's doing the mocking, and how loudly and persistently they do it, it will never tarnish even a smidgeon of the holiness, purity, and righteousness of what God does.

It's important, however, for us to keep both aspects of God's justice in mind. We usually think of what God's *against*. We also need to remember what God's *for*. The latter actually takes top priority. The former makes sense only in light of the latter.

In the garden of Eden, God was *for* innocence. Therefore, He commanded Adam to not eat from the Tree of the Knowledge of Good and Evil.

In Egypt, God was *for* the Exodus. Therefore, He commanded Pharaoh to let His people go and sent a plague each time Pharaoh said no.

At Mount Sinai, God was *for* a holy and happy people. Therefore, He gave Moses the Ten Commandments for their protection and well-being.

Like God, we pursue justice first by what we're *for*. That's one of the main reasons for reading this devotional book. The better we understand "Made by God in His Image," the better we'll understand what we're *for*. And, the better we'll live it out and model it.

May we always be known first for what we're *for* (God's way) and never first for what we're *against* (not God's way!).

Lord, Your ways are so much higher than our ways. It's so easy to be against certain things without proclaiming what I'm for. Forgive me, Father, and empower me to change.

WE TEACH KNOWLEDGE

*"To those who listen to my teaching,
more understanding will be given, and they
will have an abundance of knowledge."*
MATTHEW 13:12 NLT

What is one of the Lord's most common declarations in the Bible? He says, "you [or they] will *know* that I am the Lord." Several instances of this statement occur in Exodus. More than fifty appear in Ezekiel. Others show up in Deuteronomy, 1 Kings, Isaiah, and Joel.

In scripture, *know* can mean a lot of things. It can indicate that you heard something and forgot it just as quickly. Conversely, it can mean you heard or experienced something and want to remember it forever. That especially applies to what God says and does (truths to affirm and commands to believe). It also applies to what biblical heroes and villains say and do (examples to heed).

In God's Word, knowledge is not morally and

ethically neutral. That's why Paul says, "I want you to be wise about what is good, and innocent about what is evil" (Romans 16:19).

What's more, knowledge is not sourceless. Real knowledge always originates with God and His Word. So-called knowledge originates with the world, the flesh, and the devil. That didn't start with Eve's first bite. . .it began with everything the serpent said, untrue things that Eve and Adam decided to believe.

Furthermore, knowledge is not harmless. Jesus said the devil's evil knowledge is designed to steal, kill, and destroy (John 10:10). No wonder Satan loves to tell a truth, a half-truth, and a lie. Never fall for that trick. It's as old as the Garden and often just as deadly.

We reflect God's image when we stand for truth and teach it to others. Don't you think our world could use more men like that? Will you be one today?

Heavenly Father, people are watching and listening to me every day. Keep me strong in Your truth, and help me to teach it so others will know You are the Lord.

WE TEACH UNDERSTANDING

"To those who listen to my teaching, more understanding will be given. But for those who are not listening, even what little understanding they have will be taken away from them."

MARK 4:25 NLT

Knowledge is important, but not sufficient in itself. The Bible spurs us to go on to obtain and teach *understanding*. The half dozen biblical heroes who talk about understanding the most are Job, David, Solomon, Isaiah, Jeremiah, and Daniel. Then there is Jesus, who surpasses them all.

Near the end of his story, Job confesses: "You [God] asked, 'Who is this that obscures my plans without knowledge?' Surely I spoke of things I did not understand, things too wonderful for me to know" (Job 42:3).

Solomon advises: "Trust in the LORD with all your heart and lean not on your own understanding; in all your ways submit to him, and he will make your paths straight" (Proverbs 3:5-6).

God declares to Jeremiah: "Let the one who boasts boast about this: that they have the understanding to know me, that I am the LORD, who exercises kindness, justice and righteousness on earth, for in these I delight" (Jeremiah 9:24).

In the four Gospels, Jesus readily acknowledges the inability of people—the public, religious leaders, and even His own disciples—to understand what He was saying and doing. So after His resurrection, Jesus "opened their minds so they could understand the Scriptures" (Luke 24:45). This understanding exploded after the Holy Spirit filled Jesus' followers.

Everyone, Christian or not, bears the image of God. But we who believe and receive Jesus, who live as temples of God's Holy Spirit, can truly understand the deepest, most important issues of life. Let's always listen to Jesus' teaching, so we can receive and share even more understanding.

Lord God, what do I need to understand about You today? Please enlighten me so I can teach others Your way.

WE TEACH WISDOM

"Anyone who listens to my teaching and follows it is wise, like a person who builds a house on solid rock."
MATTHEW 7:24 NLT

Knowledge and understanding are important. But even they are not enough in themselves. God also wants us to seek His divine *wisdom*, diligently and prayerfully with His Spirit's enabling.

By *prayerfully*, we mean seeking God's wisdom through earnest communication with Him. James 1:5 says, "If any of you lacks wisdom, you should ask God, who gives generously to all without finding fault, and it will be given to you." James 3:17 calls this "wisdom that comes from heaven" and describes its very good fruit. James 5:16 (NLT) adds, "The earnest prayer of a righteous person has great power and produces wonderful results." Jesus advocated the same: "Keep on asking, and you will receive what you ask for. Keep on seeking, and you will find. Keep on knocking, and the door will be opened to you" (Matthew 7:7 NLT).

Those words, from the Lord's Sermon on the Mount, also speak to the idea of *diligence* in seeking God's wisdom. The apostle Paul, in Ephesians 1:17 says, "I keep asking that the God of our Lord Jesus Christ, the glorious Father, may give you the Spirit of wisdom and revelation, so that you may know him better." And in Colossians 1:9, Paul says, "We continually ask God to fill you with the knowledge of his will through all the wisdom and understanding that the Spirit gives."

As we know God better through His Word and prayer, we become more wise. And, like Him, we encourage others to be wise as well. In a world awash in folly, reflect God's image by teaching wisdom.

God, I need Your wisdom with Your Spirit's enabling. May Your Word find a ready home in my heart so I can encourage others to know You as well.

WE QUOTE GOD'S WORD

*It is written: "'As surely as I live,' says the
Lord, 'every knee will bow before me;
every tongue will acknowledge God.'"*
ROMANS 14:11

God loves to quote His own Word. God's Word loves to
quote itself. The Lord remembers everything He's ever
said, and biblical writers knew what previous biblical
writers had said. Therefore, God's Holy Spirit could
easily remind human beings to quote, either directly
or indirectly, earlier writings. This reinforces what was
said before and intensifies its value.

Almost every single page of the New Testament
quotes or alludes to key terms and statements from the
Hebrew scriptures. Jesus Himself demonstrated His
love for scripture, quoting it many times throughout
His public ministry.

As men made in God's image, we do well to memorize, review, and recite scripture. Why not begin with

favorite passages, Gospel verses, and key scriptures for life issues? Some people like the stately sound of the venerable King James Version, while others prefer newer translations—the New International Version, for example, is designed for ease in memorizing.

Whichever translation you read the most is probably your best bet for memorizing.

By the way, in the scripture above, the apostle Paul quoted Isaiah 45:23. A few years later, Paul alluded to Isaiah 45:23 and 66:23 when he wrote Philippians 2:10–11. God's Word is special to God. May it be special to us as well.

Lord God, help me to memorize a verse You've impressed on my heart. Then allow me to quote that scripture to someone who needs to hear it!

WE REMAIN JOYFUL

Rejoice in the Lord always.
I will say it again: Rejoice!
PHILIPPIANS 4:4

Imagine a Christian friend who dies and goes to heaven. After the initial welcome, what do you think may surprise him most about God's presence? Likely, it will be God's infinite and eternal joy.

The most joy-filled of all the New Testament letters, Philippians offers counterintuitive, heavenly-minded insights into life here on earth. Here are some possible takeaways:

Can you think of an older Christian man or some peers who serve the Lord wholeheartedly and love you well? Make a point of praying and thanking God for them daily (1:4). They'll appreciate it and your joy will abound all the more.

If you hear an unusual Christian testimony—say, of someone coming to faith after reading a secular article or listening to a worldly song—see Paul's words in 1:18 and rejoice.

Don't even let hardships or pain keep you from rejoicing in God's goodness. As Paul taught us, even death is not defeat (3:7–11). That's simply the day we meet Jesus face to face.

Never view "Made by God in His Image" as being mere duty. Paul's is the high view of ambassadorship and ministry, and therefore it's his delight to carry out fruitful labor (1:22) for "your progress and joy in the faith" (1:25). When he says "rejoice," he knows what he's talking about. . .the key is "in the Lord."

God, thank You for this reminder of Your infinite and eternal joy. May I abound in a small part of that joy today.

WE REMAIN LOYAL

*"The LORD gives his own reward for
doing good and for being loyal."*
1 SAMUEL 26:23 NLT

A lot of what we've explored in this book has been designed to spark smiles, joy, and even fun. That's the way God designed the robust, authentic, and Spirit-empowered Christian life. And for that we can be glad!

It's startling to realize the implications of God's unconditional love for us. Like the prodigal son's father, God is never disillusioned with us. He never had any illusions to begin with. If we're not careful, however, we can become disillusioned and walk away from God.

The one mistake we dare not make, author Philip Yancey reminds us, is to confuse *God* (who is good) with *life* (which is hard). Still, every Christian, at one time or another, is seriously tempted to lose his faith. Thankfully, God never abandons us. Even in the worst of circumstances, He's there, urging us to not lose hope in His goodness, greatness, and love.

Look again at today's scripture, the words of a young man who would become Israel's greatest king: David. Jesus, a descendant of David, makes a similar promise on the last page of the Bible. There He says: "See! I am coming soon. I am bringing with Me the reward I will give to everyone for what he has done" (Revelation 22:12 NLV).

Some scoff at God's offer of eternal rewards for men who remain loyal, keep doing good, and finish well. But what are your other options? Live godlessly, hurt yourself and other people, and end in utter disgrace? This is a common choice today, but no thank you!

God's image in you calls for loyalty. And His Spirit within you empowers it.

God, thank You for the rewards I can enjoy forever. Empower me always to be loyal and true to You, and to encourage other Christian men to do the same.

WE REMAIN PATIENT

Wait patiently for the LORD. Be brave and courageous. Yes, wait patiently for the LORD.
PSALM 27:14 NLT

In His lovingkindness, God is incredibly patient with fallen humanity. Instead of turning every sinner into burnt toast, He waits patiently. He doesn't want anyone to be destroyed but wants all to come to repentance.

As He waits for us, God expects us to want everyone else to come to repentance, and therefore to wait patiently. Especially when a not-yet-Christian insults or mistreats us. Instead of raging at the offender, God wants us to wait quietly on Him. Yes, it can be hard. But there's no better way to bear a fruitful harvest and rewards for all eternity.

Practically speaking, our patience includes turning the other cheek, giving the shirt and jacket off our back, going the extra mile, and sacrificing financially (Matthew 5:38–42).

In His parable of the soils, Jesus described seeds that fell on good soil, representing "honest, good-hearted people who hear God's word, cling to it, and patiently produce a huge harvest" (Luke 8:15 NLT). Are we such men? If so, our patience will produce a harvest of more souls coming to faith in Jesus Christ.

How does patience with not-yet-Christians truly result in the salvation of many? Paul explains, "Don't you see how wonderfully kind, tolerant, and patient God is with you? Does this mean nothing to you? Can't you see that his kindness is intended to turn you from your sin?" (Romans 2:4 NLT). When we show patience to those who mistreat us, we are reflecting God's image to our world. And someday, those enemies may be even better than friends—they might be brothers.

God, I've been insulted and mistreated in the past. The next time it happens, help me to remember to wait patiently on You.

WE PROTECT OUR HEARTS

Keep thy heart with all diligence;
for out of it are the issues of life.
PROVERBS 4:23 KJV

Albert Einstein was a genius, but not compared to Solomon (1 Kings 3:12). During Solomon's reign, "he was wiser than anyone else" and "his fame spread to all the surrounding nations" (1 Kings 4:31). Unfortunately, just because Solomon always knew the right thing to do doesn't mean he did it consistently.

Over the years, Solomon penned many observations about the realities of life. His writings include two psalms (Psalms 72 and 127), hundreds of proverbs (Proverbs 1–29), a poetic essay (Ecclesiastes), and a musical (Song of Songs). Yet even though wisdom flowed from Solomon's pen, he started growing cynical and, much later, finally put down his pen, turned his back on the Lord, worshipped man-made idols, and finished life as an old fool.

How could the man who had it all figured out in his *head* end up missing it so badly in real life?

Today's scripture aptly explains Solomon's own foolish downfall. With each foreign wife that Solomon added to his harem, his *heart* drifted farther from the Lord (1 Kings 11). Yes, Solomon knew the Lord's specific command not to marry foreign women, let alone worship their false gods. Yet it isn't enough simply to know. Solomon let his guard down, polluted his heart, and in most areas of life blew it, badly.

As men, made in God's image, we must keep our heads *and* our hearts in line with His word and will. Protect your heart with all diligence. Your life depends on it.

God, I don't want to blow it badly. Please help me to make a firm commitment to reading, studying, and applying Your Word regularly.

WE SACRIFICE FOR OUR FAMILIES

Enjoy life with your wife, whom you love, all the days. . .that God has given you under the sun. . . . For this is your lot in life and in your toilsome labor under the sun. Whatever your hand finds to do, do it with all your might.

ECCLESIASTES 9:9–10

As "Made by God in His Image" Christian men, we know the value and satisfaction of working hard to support our families. But our circumstances can be very different from man to man, family to family, community to community.

One man's son has serious birth defects. Insurance helps, but certainly doesn't begin to cover all the costs. Now, he's taken a second job to make ends meet. His wife calls him a hero.

Another man works long hours at his day job, then does a lot of freelance work on the side. He wants to be a good dad by providing for his family—but as his kids grow up, they grumble about their workaholic father.

Clearly, the number of hours worked isn't the gauge of a good Christian man—it's the heart behind hours worked. "Sacrifice" in the first man's case is scratching out the money needed to keep his family fed, clothed, and sheltered. For the second guy, sacrifice may be foregoing some of that extra money so he can spend more quality time with his wife and children.

Money is never the measure of a man. As Jesus Himself taught, "Watch out! Be on your guard against all kinds of greed; life does not consist in an abundance of possessions" (Luke 12:15). The apostle Paul added that "the love of money is a root of all kinds of evil. Some people, eager for money, have wandered from the faith and pierced themselves with many griefs" (1 Timothy 6:10). But there's no doubt that money is important, and a Christian man who doesn't provide for his family is "worse than an unbeliever" (1 Timothy 5:8).

No matter our circumstance, we sacrifice for our family because God sacrificed for us. Pray that He will guide you into the proper balance of time spent on work and family.

God, now more than ever, I need Your wisdom in knowing how best to sacrifice for my family. Your will be done, not my own.

WE SACRIFICE FOR GOD'S CHURCH

"Give, and it will be given to you. A good measure, pressed down, shaken together and running over, will be poured into your lap. For with the measure you use, it will be measured to you."

LUKE 6:38

Imagine you have only eighty dollars left to pay eight hundred dollars' worth of bills. What's the only thing a wholehearted lover of God can do in such a circumstance? Put it in the offering at church. Give it all. Don't hold anything back. And then don't be one bit surprised when God blesses you with an anonymous gift of 830 dollars. Not 800 dollars, but 830. . .because He remembered you also needed some gas money.

That's the way God works. He expects us as Christian men to give to His work on earth. But then He turns around and blesses us, over and above what we "gave up" for Him.

God loves His church, the worldwide assembly of every true believer in Jesus. And He's called many people to work in and for that church, whether pastors, evangelists, missionaries, or any of the countless support team members who keep the wheels turning. As a man made in God's image, love His church like He does by giving, sacrificially, to its support.

Jesus commended a poor widow who put her last two coins into the temple treasury. Other people had made big, ostentatious offerings, but Jesus said, "Truly I tell you, this poor widow has put more into the treasury than all the others. They all gave out of their wealth; but she, out of her poverty, put in everything—all she had to live on" (Mark 12:43-44). Though the Gospel account ends there, don't imagine for a second that God didn't make up that woman's generous giving in any number of ways—financially, spiritually, relationally, you name it.

How easily we ignore this marvelous truth: Everything—everything—we desire, want, and need is found in the Lord, and through the Lord alone. Why would we look anywhere else?

God, I want to love You wholeheartedly.
And today I want to love others well.
May I experience and overflow with Your
sacrificial, generous, giving love today.

WE SACRIFICE FOR THE NEEDY

*Each of you should give what you have
decided in your heart to give, not reluctantly
or under compulsion, for God loves a cheerful
giver. And God is able to bless you abundantly,
so that in all things at all times, having all that
you need, you will abound in every good work.*

2 CORINTHIANS 9:7–8

We can't help it. We wince every time we see someone who's poor and needy. We don't want to throw money away supporting who knows what addictions they might have.

Then again, Jesus Himself knew what it was like to be homeless. He spent the better part of three years depending on the charity of others (Matthew 8:20, Luke 8:1-3, and Luke 9:58).

Having received this kind of assistance, Jesus and His disciples spent their time and energy preaching the Gospel to the poor (Matthew 5:3, 11:5, Luke 4:18,

6:20, 7:22, and John 12:5). And, if we read between the lines of the story of Jesus' anointing in Bethany, it appears that He and His team regularly gave money to the poor (Matthew 26:9, Mark 14:5, and John 13:29).

Of course, Jesus didn't just give of His leftovers. As the apostle Paul described it, "you know the grace of our Lord Jesus Christ, that though he was rich, yet for your sake he became poor, so that you through his poverty might become rich" (2 Corinthians 8:9).

To us Christian men made in God's image, it's no wonder that Jesus promised eternal blessings for caring for the homeless and destitute (Matthew 19:21, 25:31-40, Mark 10:21, Luke 11:41, 12:33, 14:13, 18:22, and 19:8-9).

The needy are all around you. Look for tangible ways you can meet their needs. And don't worry about the ways they might misuse your gift. Instead, consider how the Lord might use it to bring them to Himself.

God, it's so easy to misjudge the needy. Yet Jesus' example is crystal clear. Help me to open my wallet and sacrifice for the poor people You bring across my path.

WE SHARE "GOOD NEWS"

*How beautiful on the mountains are the feet
of him who brings good news, who tells of
peace and brings good news of happiness.*
ISAIAH 52:7 NLV

Imagine watching the Lord God create Adam from the dust of the earth. The Lord then breathes the breath of life into him. Adam sits up, takes several deep breaths, and laughs. "What just happened?" The Lord Jesus helps him to his feet, introduces Himself, and goes for His first walk with Adam in the cool of the evening.

During that walk, Adam repeatedly expresses his wonder and delight. Then the Lord focuses His eyes on his and says, "The good news is that this is all yours to enjoy and share."

The Old Testament mentions "good news" more than a dozen times and the New Testament uses the terms "good news" and "Gospel" more than 120 times. General good news is always welcome. . .but that's nothing compared to the transforming power of the life-changing Gospel of Jesus Christ.

Here's some perspective: during the ministry of the prophet Elisha, everyone in the city of Samaria was being starved to death by the massive Aramean army. Four lepers who were near death discovered that the enemy camp was completely deserted—and full of food. After feasting awhile, they said to each other, "What we're doing is not right. This is a day of good news and we are keeping it to ourselves" (2 Kings 7:9). How much more right it is to share the good news of Jesus Christ! We dare not keep it to ourselves. Jesus shared it wherever He went, and He sent His disciples two by two to do the same.

God gives good gifts (James 1:17), the most amazing and perfect gift being His Son, Jesus Christ (John 3:16). Reflect His image by passing that good news on to others around you. They—and you—will be eternally blessed.

God, I will look for opportunities today to mention the "good news" to people. You do the rest, please.

WE SAY "BLESS YOU"

Just then Boaz arrived from Bethlehem and greeted the harvesters, "The LORD be with you!" "The LORD bless you!" they answered.

RUTH 2:4

God blessed Adam and Eve (Genesis 1:22, 1:28, and 5:2). God blessed Noah and his sons (Genesis 9:1). The first time scripture records God actually saying "I will bless you" is in Genesis 12:2–3, when He spoke to Abraham.

Conversely, the first time scripture records a man saying, in essence, "You are blessed by God," appears in Genesis 14:18–20, when Melchizedek ("priest of God Most High") blessed God's friend, Abraham.

What starts with Abraham, the father of God's people, continues with God blessing each successive patriarch and each patriarch either blessing his sons or asking God to bless them.

This blessing cycle happens because we are made in God's image. He blesses us, we bless others, and the goodness goes around and around.

Now, just to be clear, we're not discussing the throw-away comment so many of us make after another person sneezes! Real, biblical blessings involve us speaking truth over others. We encourage and challenge them to know, follow, and serve God. We urge them to stay true to their faith and offer words of guidance for the future. The most important part of the blessing, as we see in today's scripture from Ruth, is that it's "the LORD" underlying all.

We don't have to be stingy or miserly in blessing others. Just the opposite. The more we say "Bless you" or "God bless you" to others, the better. Over coffee and a snack. When you're done meeting with someone. When you sacrificially help a needy person. Opportunities abound for men to reflect the blessed (and blessing) image of God.

Father in heaven, I want to be much more generous and frequent in blessing others and saying "God bless you!"

WE SAY "FEAR NOT"

And the LORD, he it is that doth go before thee;
he will be with thee, he will not fail thee, neither
forsake thee: fear not, neither be dismayed.
DEUTERONOMY 31:8 KJV

Contrary to popular belief, "fear not" and related phrases don't appear in the Bible 365 times. Then again, how often does the Bible have to say something to prove its importance? Some 95 to 115 times (depending on the Bible translation) should be sufficient, right?

In Genesis 15:1, God tells Abraham, "Do not be afraid." God says the same thing to Hagar, Isaac, and Jacob in Genesis 21:17, 26:24 and 46:3. God spoke the same words to Moses (Numbers 21:34), Joshua (Joshua 1:9), Gideon (Judges 6:23), Jeremiah (Jeremiah 1:8), and others. Meanwhile, godly men of scripture spoke the same words to the fearful people around them. Joseph told his brothers twice (Genesis 50:19–21). Moses said it to the Israelites, right before the Lord drowned the

Egyptian army (Exodus 14:13). Moses said the words again, right after the Lord gave him the Ten Commandments (Exodus 20:20), and continued saying the same thing through the end of Deuteronomy. Then Joshua picked up the torch.

In the four Gospels, Jesus repeatedly said, "Don't be afraid" or "Do not be afraid." And notice that He never said this to someone who was enjoying peace, calm, and ease. No—Jesus was saying this to individuals whose lives had been torn apart.

The bottom line for us is that God wants us to trust Him. There is no need for fear. Then, because we're made in His image and enjoying His peace, He wants us to come alongside people in crisis and say, "Don't be afraid. Trust God. Keep your eyes and heart fixed on Him."

Lord God, it's not hard to find people in crisis. Please help me to listen as long as it takes, and then tell him, "Don't be afraid. Trust God."

WE SAY "I'M WITH YOU"

" 'Do what you think is best,' the armor bearer replied. 'I'm with you completely, whatever you decide.' "

1 Samuel 14:7 NLT

In every sphere of life, we need someone who echoes today's scripture: "I'm with you completely, whatever you decide." That's true in family, among friends, with a colleague at work, at church, in the community, wherever. Of course, it doesn't mean they're physically with you every moment. But when you need him, he's there with you in spirit, ready to listen, ready to support.

Sometimes "I'm with you" lasts for a particular season of life. Sometimes it lasts for multiple seasons. How blessed is the man who has one, two, or three brothers in Christ who pledge to stick with him through everything. That's exactly the way God deals with us. As the writer of Hebrews says, "God has said, 'Never will I leave you; never will I forsake you' " (Hebrews 13:5).

So be like God, reflecting His faithfulness. Let a friend know "I'm with you" for this particular season of life. And then, as God leads, renew that pledge during the next season or two. Trust God to lead your friend to make the same pledge to you.

Embrace the apostle Paul's words, "Because we loved you so much, we were delighted to share with you not only the gospel of God but our lives as well" (1 Thessalonians 2:8).

We live in a hard world, a place where people and events conspire to depress and even destroy us. But God foresaw that and gave us friends. "Two are better than one," the writer of Ecclesiastes said, "because they have a good return for their labor. If either of them falls down, one can help the other up. But pity anyone who falls and has no one to help them up" (Ecclesiastes 4:9–10).

Say "I'm with you." And back it up with action.

God, I'll make a point of telling my closest Christian brothers that "I'm with you." And I'll trust You to make our bond even closer.

WE SAY "WELL DONE"

"You have done well. You are a good and faithful servant. You have been faithful over a few things. I will put many things in your care. Come and share my joy."

MATTHEW 25:21, 25:23 NLV

A slight nod of the head may be a positive non-verbal, but all men need to hear "I love you," "I'm proud of you," and "Well done!" How many of us have heard those words, especially from our fathers? And when we do hear such words, do we sometimes wonder, "Do they really mean that?"

Men often struggle to verbalize their feelings. But since we're made in the image of the God who is love (1 John 4:8), let's ask Him for strength to speak these words of affirmation over the guys in our life—our fathers or sons, our friends or coworkers, our pastors or fellow church members. God speaks words of love all through His Word (see Jeremiah 31:3, John 13:34,

Revelation 3:9), words that should encourage our own hearts and through us encourage other guys.

Why is it that so many guys can shout and cheer for a professional athlete but find it tougher to express intentional, heartfelt praise for relatives and friends? If this is true of you, to whatever extent, know that Christian life is all about growth. . .and God will be happy to help you improve in this area too.

Jesus has told us what He wants to say when we first arrive in heaven: "Well done!" Also expect to hear "I love you" and "I'm proud of you" more than a few times. Just a few choice words, spoken from the heart, can change everything for the better.

Let's be like Jesus and His Father, who speak words of affirmation over their own. Are you thinking of ways you can do this? Well done!

God, I thank You for loving me as much as You do. Now help me to express love to others.

WE SAY "YES"

For no matter how many promises God has made,
they are "Yes" in Christ. And so through him the
"Amen" is spoken by us to the glory of God.

2 CORINTHIANS 1:20

How many times has God said "Yes" to you? Think about this: God said "Yes" to creating you. He said "Yes" to keeping you alive. He said "Yes" to your knowing Him. He said "Yes" to you receiving and reading His Word. He said "Yes" to you hearing the good news of Jesus Christ and saying "Yes" in return. And in many other ways, God has said "Yes" to you.

Jesus taught that God loves to say "Yes" to our prayers, spoken in His name and for His glory. "I will do whatever you ask in my name, so that the Father may be glorified in the Son," He said (John 14:13). "I chose you and appointed you so that you might go and bear fruit—fruit that will last—and so that whatever you ask in my name the Father will give you" (John 15:16). After all, Jesus said another time, "If you, then, though you are evil, know how to give good gifts to your children, how much more will your Father in heaven give good gifts to those who ask him!" (Matthew 7:11). We could probably even suppose that some of the times God has said "No" to us, He was actually saying "Yes" to something better.

Because we are made in His image, let's be "yes men"—guys who always say "Yes" to what He calls us to do. And let's say "Yes" as often as possible to family, friends, neighbors, and coworkers. Sure, there are times we'll need to say "No". . .but often, saying "Yes" gives us an opportunity to share God's love with someone who needs it.

What could be more positive than that?

God, I gladly and repeatedly say "Yes" and "Amen" to Your glory, honor, and praise—now privately, and soon publicly.

WE PROVE COURAGEOUS

*"Study this Book of Instruction continually.
Meditate on it day and night so you will be sure
to obey everything written in it. Only then will
you prosper and succeed in all you do. This is
my command—be strong and courageous! Do
not be afraid or discouraged. For the LORD
your God is with you wherever you go."*

JOSHUA 1:8–9 NLT

Every time we give in to fear, we need to humbly acknowledge it, remind ourselves what we should do the next time, then move toward that "next time" as quickly as possible. This is true in every sphere of life . . .and our success begins with a biblical understanding of who God is and what He has to say about fearing Him and no one else.

First, fear God most. There is an aspect of fright in this fear, since He is so infinitely beyond us in His holiness. But our fear of God is also a reverent awe for the One who loved us enough to send His Son,

Jesus, to pay for our sins. We can approach this God courageously, without wavering or doubting (Matthew 21:21, Mark 9:24, Romans 4:20-22, Hebrews 10:23, and Jude 21).

Next, we show courage by continually doing what is good and right (Genesis 22:1, Psalm 106:31, 2 Corinthians 1:24, Galatians 5:6, Philippians 1:25, Colossians 2:7, 2 Thessalonians 1:3, and James 2:14). The God who made us, whose image we reflect, will empower us to do whatever He calls us to do.

As God's image bearers, we must never fear what others might do (2 Chronicles 20:15, Nehemiah 4:14, Psalm 118:6, Isaiah 8:13 and Matthew 10:28). We can limit our fear to God alone, trusting His goodness no matter what happens (2 Thessalonians 1:4-5, 2 Timothy 2:3, Hebrews 10:35-36, James 1:3, 5:11, 1 Peter 1:5-7, 5:8-11, and Revelation 2:10).

There's no greater example of courage than Jesus, who left the glories of heaven to live—and die—as a man on this earth. As the time of His crucifixion neared, "Jesus resolutely set out for Jerusalem" (Luke 9:51). Allow God the Father, through His Holy Spirit, to make you more like Jesus the Son.

God, Your Word says "be strong and courageous!" I wholeheartedly agree. As I face hardships and setbacks, I will trust You rather than fearing my circumstances.

WE PROVE FULLY COMMITTED

"The eyes of the LORD search the whole earth in order to strengthen those whose hearts are fully committed to him."
2 CHRONICLES 16:9 NLT

Who can say he's "fully committed" to God? Surprisingly, all of us can. We simply need to ask for God's strength to be fully committed. How frequently? At least daily. God will be happy to pour His power into the image bearer who makes the request.

Half a dozen power-packed scriptures penned by Paul show us the way.

First, "I pray that out of [our heavenly Father's] glorious riches he may strengthen you with power through his Spirit in your inner being" (Ephesians 3:16).

Second, Paul affirmed, "I can do all this through him [Christ] who gives me strength" (Philippians 4:13).

Third, Paul prayed for believers to "live a life worthy of the Lord and please him in every way: bearing fruit in every good work, growing in the knowledge of God, being strengthened with all power according to his glorious might so that you may have great endurance and patience, and giving joyful thanks to the Father" (Colossians 1:10–12).

Fourth, "So then, just as you received Christ Jesus as Lord, continue to live your lives in him, rooted and built up in him, strengthened in the faith as you were taught, and overflowing with thankfulness" (Colossians 2:6–7).

Fifth, "May he [the Lord] strengthen your hearts so that you will be blameless and holy in the presence of our God and Father when our Lord Jesus comes with all his holy ones" (1 Thessalonians 3:13).

Finally, "May our Lord Jesus Christ himself and God our Father, who loved us and by his grace gave us eternal encouragement and good hope, encourage your hearts and strengthen you in every good deed and word" (2 Thessalonians 2:16–17).

The successful Christian life always looks forward, not back (Luke 9:62). God wants you to make a full commitment, and He'll help you to do it. How can you possibly lose?

God, yes, it's true. Each day I need to ask for Your strength and power to be fully committed to You. This is today's request.

WE ENJOY GOD'S PEACE

*"Salt is good for seasoning. But if it loses
its flavor, how do you make it salty again?
You must have the qualities of salt among
yourselves and live in peace with each other."*
MARK 9:50 NLT

In the presence of God the Father, God the Son, and God the Holy Spirit is infinite, eternal peace. The Trinity never panics, struggles, wrestles, or anguishes. God never feels agitated, disturbed, or conflicted.

In heaven, there are no emergencies. The angels aren't rushing around. The presence of God is always surrounded by infinite, eternal peace.

How good that, every day, we can experience a small part of His perfect peace (Isaiah 26:3) that passes all understanding (Philippians 4:7).

Prayers for peace dot the pages of the New Testament. The apostle Paul often asked God to grant peace to the people in his letters. So did Peter, John, and Jude. That clearly suggests that peace is one of the most important gifts we can offer each other as Christian brothers. No wonder God, in the words of Paul, wants us to "live in peace with each other" (1 Thessalonians 5:13).

Granted, not everyone wants peace. Some people thrive on conflict and chaos. God knows that, and His Spirit inspired the Bible writers to address the problem realistically. "Do all that *you* can," Paul wrote, "to live in peace with everyone" (Romans 12:18 NLT, emphasis added).

You were made in God's image. God Himself is peaceful. And having been "justified through faith," you have "peace with God through our Lord Jesus Christ" (Romans 5:1). Enjoy the peace. Share it with others.

God, I'm going to take a few minutes
right now to rest in Your presence
and quietly soak up Your peace.

WE THRIVE IN GOD'S GOODNESS, PART 1

*What shall I return to the LORD
for all his goodness to me?*
PSALM 116:12

In heaven, the Lord God thrives in His own goodness. That goodness includes His infinite and eternal holiness and love. God's goodness here on earth is seen in His purposeful guidance, providential care, and specific answers to prayers. The more we enjoy these good gifts, the more we feel "Made by God in His Image." Many scriptures celebrate this.

Psalm 84:11 says, "The LORD God is a sun and shield; the LORD bestows favor and honor; no good thing does he withhold from those whose walk is blameless."

We can always trust that God has our best interest at heart: "We know that in all things God works for the good of those who love him, who have been called according to his purpose" (Romans 8:28).

"Do not conform to the pattern of this world, but be transformed by the renewing of your mind," Romans 12:2 urges. Why? "Then you will be able to test and approve what God's will is—his good, pleasing and perfect will."

And God's will is that we Christian men, made in His image, do good as He is good. "We are God's handiwork, created in Christ Jesus to do good works, which God prepared in advance for us to do" (Ephesians 2:10). "For it is God who works in you to will and to act in order to fulfill his good purpose" (Philippians 2:13).

It is encouraging and exciting to know that God's goodness surrounds and empowers us. What can you return to the Lord for all His goodness to you?

God, You alone are good. Thank You so much for Your goodness, which makes me thrive at doing good works that will count for all eternity.

WE THRIVE IN GOD'S GOODNESS, PART 2

God can give you all you need. He will give you more than enough. You will have everything you need for yourselves. And you will have enough left over to give when there is a need.

2 CORINTHIANS 9:8 NLV

As we saw yesterday, God's goodness here on earth is seen in His purposeful guidance, providential care, and specific answers to prayers. The more we enjoy these good gifts, the more we feel "Made by God in His Image."

Here are a few more scriptures that celebrate God's goodness.

Second Chronicles 6:41 reads, "May your priests, LORD God, be clothed with salvation, may your faithful people rejoice in your goodness." As Christian men, we have every reason to rejoice in the Lord's goodness every day.

The apostle Paul, in 2 Thessalonians 1:11 wrote, "With this in mind, we constantly pray for you, that our God may make you worthy of his calling, and that by his power he may bring to fruition your every desire for goodness and your every deed prompted by faith." Imagine personalizing this prayer for your closest Christian friends and loved ones!

Paul again, in 2 Timothy 3:16–17, taught that "all Scripture is God-breathed and is useful for teaching, rebuking, correcting and training in righteousness, so that the servant of God may be thoroughly equipped for every good work." God's inspired Word is a wonderful source of His infinite and eternal goodness. Be sure to spend time with it regularly.

And finally, the apostle Peter said that God's "divine power has given us everything we need for a godly life through our knowledge of him who called us by his own glory and goodness" (2 Peter 1:3). God's goodness is our power for successful living.

God, You have done everything so I can thrive in Your goodness. Thank You. May I in turn pass along Your goodness to others.

WE THRIVE IN GOD'S GREATNESS

*"Yours, L*ORD*, is the greatness and the power and the glory and the majesty and the splendor, for everything in heaven and earth is yours. Yours, L*ORD*, is the kingdom; you are exalted as head over all."*

1 CHRONICLES 29:11

Did you know the Lord's Prayer in Matthew 6 ends with an extra sentence in the King James Version? That extra sentence says, "For thine is the kingdom, and the power, and the glory, for ever. Amen." Newer translations tend to move that extra sentence into a footnote. That's because it doesn't appear in the oldest New Testament Greek manuscripts.

But it's certainly not wrong—and actually very good—to include this extra sentence when we recite the Lord's Prayer. If you haven't memorized Matthew 6:9-13 yet, do so today. And if you haven't incorporated the Lord's Prayer into your daily prayers, decide today whether to recite it aloud at a specific time, say breakfast or dinner.

After all, the Lord's Prayer begins with God the Father's greatness. Matthew 6:9–10 says, "Our Father in heaven, hallowed be your name, your kingdom come, your will be done, on earth as it is in heaven."

Those two verses, and the extra sentence noted above, directly echo today's scripture. Reading and reciting these words aloud often provokes a sense of awe at God's transcendent greatness. Without question, the Creator and Maker of heaven and earth is Lord of all. . .and the amazing thing is that He's shared that greatness with us. Made in His image, we reflect His incredible glory, however faultily. But remade by His Son, Jesus Christ, we reflect Him in ever-increasing glory (2 Corinthians 3:18).

God's infinite and eternal greatness knows no rival. His greatness and goodness bless us beyond measure!

God, thank You so much for Your greatness and goodness, which indeed bless me beyond measure. I am humbled to be made in Your great image.

WE ENJOY HUMOR

. . .a time to weep and a time to laugh.
ECCLESIASTES 3:4

The Bible only portrays God laughing in a negative way: that is, in response to the puny opposition of humanity (Psalm 2:4, 37:13, 59:8). But we can read between the lines of scripture to surmise that God does indeed have a sense of humor. Try this: read the book of Jonah aloud for fun. The prophet's irrationality can produce laugh-out-loud moments.

Another Old Testament prophet engaged in a bit of sarcasm in his contest with the prophets of Baal. "About noontime Elijah began mocking them. 'You'll have to shout louder,' he scoffed, 'for surely he is a god! Perhaps he is daydreaming, or is relieving himself. Or maybe he is away on a trip, or is asleep and needs to be wakened!'" (1 Kings 18:27 NLT).

And how could God *not* enjoy humor and laughter when Proverbs 15:15 reads, "The cheerful heart has a continual feast," and Proverbs 17:22 says, "A cheerful heart is good medicine."

As "Made by God in His Image" men, we have a sense of humor. It's why we love comedies, cartoons, and joking with friends. When we tease and goof around, however, the challenge is knowing where to draw the line.

The apostle Paul sent guidelines to the Christians of Ephesus, rules that come down through the centuries to us as well: "Among you there must not be even a hint of sexual immorality, or of any kind of impurity, or of greed, because these are improper for God's holy people. Nor should there be obscenity, foolish talk or coarse joking, which are out of place, but rather thanksgiving" (Ephesians 5:3-4).

For as serious as His mission was, it's hard to imagine Jesus as a sour, dour individual. . .especially considering His interactions with little children (Mark 10:13-15). He probably shared many good laughs with His disciples. Let's do the same with our family and friends. . .but just be sure it's a *good* laugh.

Lord God, I thank You for laughter.
May I always combine my laughter
with gratitude for all of Your good gifts.

WE TREASURE GOD'S WORD

*I rejoice in your word like one
who discovers a great treasure.*
PSALM 119:162 NLT

God's Word is relevant to all men, everywhere, and at all times. According to 2 Timothy 3:16–17, all scripture is inspired by God and is useful, profitable, beneficial, practical, and full of rewards for the person who treasures it. As men made in His image, let's be sure His Word fills our hearts and minds.

There's no secret code or formula for treasuring the Bible. The world's best seller is written so people hearing or reading it can quickly grasp what God is saying to them. Of course, you may not catch *everything* the first time through. It's human nature to listen to a favorite song over and over again or to watch a sports replay when you already know the game result. And it's absolutely okay to stop and reread passages in scripture. In fact, it's more than just okay. . .it's a great idea!

As you read and study your Bible, keep asking yourself, *What did God mean by this?* If you're not sure, give yourself time. Do your best to discover what God wants you to know, even if that takes a few (or several) readings. Most of the rewards will be right there in His Word, paid off by your persistence. The Lord does want you to know what He's saying.

In the end, though, you may still have unanswered questions. In some cases, you'll have to wait until heaven to ask Moses, David, Daniel, or Paul, "What did you mean by that?" Imagine how interesting and fun that will be.

Even more amazing will be living in the presence of Jesus, the Word of God, who died to pay the price for your sins. Treasure Him!

Lord God, I am grateful for Your written Word, and the living Word, Jesus Christ. You have been so generous. Thank You for this incredible treasure.

WE TREASURE GOD'S WAYS

Lay not up for yourselves treasures upon earth, where moth and rust doth corrupt, and where thieves break through and steal: but lay up for yourselves treasures in heaven, where neither moth nor rust doth corrupt, and where thieves do not break through nor steal: for where your treasure is, there will your heart be also.

MATTHEW 6:19–21 KJV

Knowledge, understanding, and especially wisdom are important, but still not enough. Ultimately, God wants us to go on to know and treasure His *ways* more than anything else men usually prize here on earth.

No other treasure is harder to find. The prophet Isaiah said, "Truly, O God of Israel, our Savior, you work in mysterious ways" (45:15 NLT). And the apostle Paul marveled, "Oh, how great are God's riches and wisdom and knowledge! How impossible it is for us to understand his decisions and his ways!" (Romans 11:33 NLT).

Thankfully, God makes some of those mysterious ways known to us—that's what the Bible is all about. As the apostle Peter said, God's "divine power has given us everything we need for a godly life through our knowledge of him who called us by his own glory and goodness. Through these he has given us his very great and precious promises" (2 Peter 1:3-4).

The Bible writer James goes on to say: "If you are wise and understand God's ways, prove it by living an honorable life, doing good works with the humility that comes from wisdom" (James 3:13 NLT). The more we treasure God's ways and live by them, the more of His ways God will reveal to us, and the greater will be His image shining through us.

One day in heaven, multitudes will sing the song of Moses and God's perfect Lamb: "Great and marvelous are your works, O Lord God, the Almighty. Just and true are your ways, O King of the nations" (Revelation 15:3 NLT). Like them, we want to enthusiastically praise and treasure God's ways, both now and in glory.

God, yes, I want to treasure Your ways more than anything this world offers. To treasure Your ways is to draw closer to Your heart. I truly want to be Your friend.

WE SPEAK TRUTH

*"I have not spoken in secret, from somewhere
in a land of darkness; I have not said to Jacob's
descendants, 'Seek me in vain.' I, the LORD,
speak the truth; I declare what is right."*

ISAIAH 45:19

In a world of falsehood, it's good to know there is an objective truth. Since God created everything, He is the standard by which all other things are measured. And He assures us that He speaks truth.

Jesus Christ, the second person of the Trinity and the sacrifice for sin, described Himself as "the way and the truth and the life" (John 14:6).

And the Holy Spirit is called "the Spirit of truth" by Jesus, who said He "will guide you into all the truth" (John 16:13).

Our God is a truth-speaker, and men who are made in His image should be as well. In fact, honesty is chiseled into the most basic laws of human experience, the Ten Commandments: "You shall not give false testimony against your neighbor" (Exodus 20:16).

God actually loathes dishonesty. Proverbs 6:16–19 describes "six things the LORD hates, seven that are detestable to him," and that list includes "a lying tongue." Judgment is promised to "all liars" (Revelation 21:8), those who practice deceit (21:27), and "love" falsehood (22:15). Our call to truthfulness couldn't be plainer.

Modern culture, which seems to enjoy being lied to, will push us to "fudge" the truth in our relationships, at our workplaces, and on our taxes. But to reflect God's image, we need to be impeccably honest. If you feel the temptation to be otherwise, here's a prayer of David to recite: "Teach me Your way, O Lord. I will walk in Your truth. May my heart fear Your name" (Psalm 86:11 NLV).

Lord God, this world doesn't encourage truthfulness, but You demand it. As I commit to speaking the truth, please empower me to do so. . .in love.

WE SPEAK WISELY

We do, however, speak a message of wisdom among the mature, but not the wisdom of this age or of the rulers of this age, who are coming to nothing.

1 CORINTHIANS 2:6

If a child says she hates homework, it tells you one thing. It's another thing if a friend or family member tells you he doesn't believe the Bible—in fact, he distrusts it and doesn't want to read it anymore. That sounds like a hatred of God's Word, and that may be the case. More often, however, what that guy is saying—even if he doesn't realize it—is that he's rejecting the distorted, false images of the Bible that he's picked up from misguided family members, coworkers, teachers, or media personalities.

If a child says he hates broccoli, it tells you one thing. It's another thing if a graduate student tells you she doesn't love God anymore —in fact she hates God and doesn't want anything to do with Him. It sounds like she hates the God of the Bible—the God who made heaven and earth—and that may be the case. More often, however, what she's saying—even if she doesn't have the wisdom to realize it—is that she's rejecting the distorted, repulsive, false images of "God" that she's been exposed to in her university classes.

Wise Christian men listen carefully to such complaints, but don't take them literally or respond quickly. In that way, they reflect God Himself. Recall that He heard out the complaints of His own people like Job and Habakkuk. And Jesus suffered the abuse of the two criminals hanging on crosses beside His. But in time, through the Father's wise and patient words, both Job and Habakkuk came to grasp more fully who He is. And over the course of three hours on the cross, one of those criminals heard Jesus' gentle, helpful, forgiving words and came to salvation.

Let's commit ourselves to wise, patient, honorable talk. It will please God and benefit our fellow man.

God, thank You that You don't believe everything I say rashly. You hear me and wait. May I wisely do the same.

WE'RE SLOW TO ANGER

A man's understanding makes him slow to anger. It is to his honor to forgive and forget a wrong done to him.
PROVERBS 19:11 NLV

When the Lord declares His name—who He is—He frequently talks about how He is slow to anger. We see this clearly in Exodus 34:6. The idea is echoed in Numbers 14:18, Nehemiah 9:17, Psalm 86:15, 103:8, 145:8, Joel 2:13, Jonah 4:2, and Nahum 1:3.

And God wants us, as men made in His image, to be slow to anger as well. With whom? With everyone—including those who hurt us financially, harangue us at work, mock us for our faith, and harm us in any number of other ways.

Burning with anger against our fellow man leads only to more sin. Psalm 37:8 says, "Refrain from anger and turn from wrath; do not fret—it leads only to evil." When you feel angry (and you will sometimes), don't say anything. As Proverbs 15:1 teaches, "A gentle answer turns away wrath, but a harsh word stirs up anger."

As we follow God and His Word, we enjoy His wonderful favor throughout our lives. Psalm 30:4-5 tells us, "Sing the praises of the LORD, you his faithful people; praise his holy name. For his anger lasts only a moment, but his favor lasts a lifetime; weeping may stay for the night, but rejoicing comes in the morning."

If you're prone to anger, and most men are, ask God to change you thoroughly. When Colossians 3:8 tells you to "rid yourselves of all such things as these: anger, rage, malice, slander, and filthy language from your lips," the command must be achievable. What God wants in your life, He'll enable.

Finally, in all things, love. God's kind of love "does not dishonor others, it is not self-seeking, it is not easily angered, it keeps no record of wrongs" (1 Corinthians 13:5).

Lord, I know that anger is common
but it can also be ugly. Please forgive me.
Please make me slow to anger, like Yourself.

WE SEEK GOD'S GLORY

For God, who said, "Let light shine out of darkness," made his light shine in our hearts to give us the light of the knowledge of God's glory displayed in the face of Christ.

2 CORINTHIANS 4:6

If we want to seek God's glory, we'll need to look for it in the face of Jesus Christ. Colossians 1:15 says, "The Son is the image of the invisible God." Hebrews 1:3 adds, "The Son is the radiance of God's glory." When we focus our spiritual pursuits on Jesus Himself, it brings great joy to the Trinity!

We clearly see God's glory in the face of Jesus on the Mount of Transfiguration. Matthew 17:2 says, "There [Jesus] was transfigured before them. His face shone like the sun, and his clothes became as white as the light." Let's always remember that Jesus Christ is fully God and two thousand years ago became fully human. Now, God the Father is remaking us in the image of His Son.

When we see Jesus in person someday, God's glory will radiate from His face and entire being. Revelation 1:16 says, "In [Jesus'] right hand he held seven stars, and coming out of his mouth was a sharp, double-edged sword. His face was like the sun shining in all its brilliance."

At that moment, we too will be transfigured. "Dear friends," John wrote, "now we are children of God, and what we will be has not yet been made known. But we know that when Christ appears, we shall be like him, for we shall see him as he is" (1 John 3:2).

At that point, the brokenness that mars God's image in us will be gone, permanently. What a day that will be!

God, may I see the face of Jesus more clearly as I read the Gospels now and in the future. Please remake me more and more into His image.

WE SEEK GOD'S HONOR

Then those who feared the LORD talked with each other, and the LORD listened and heard. A scroll of remembrance was written in his presence concerning those who feared the LORD and honored his name.
MALACHI 3:16

Throughout biblical history, men did most anything to gain glory and honor for themselves. What are we to think of forbidden fruit and murder, battles and wars, epic quests and tall tales, statues and monuments, enhanced names and absurd decrees? Weren't they pursued in a vain attempt to satisfy some man's over-sized ego?

Only God can declare His own honor. To do otherwise would be to bear false witness, mislead, and lie, which God cannot do (Titus 1:2). So, the Father delights in honoring His Son and the Holy Spirit. Jesus always seeks the honor of His Father and the Holy Spirit, who in turn gladly honors the Father and Son. Like the Trinity, "Made by God in His Image" men always seek God's honor, not their own.

True, certain honors will come to us in this life. We should welcome and receive them. But when that happens, let's say thank you, point to heaven, and publicly reflect the glory back to our Lord. To honor ourselves is pride, and pride is devastating. Pride was what caused Satan to fall in the first place. Pride, the desire to be "like God," tripped up Adam and Eve (Genesis 3:1–7). Pride, according to the Proverbs, "goes before destruction" and "a haughty spirit before a fall" (16:18).

But we, as God's image bearers, never need to stumble. His biblical formula for us is clear: Be humble. Always seek to honor Him. And, in due time, let Him honor you.

Lord God, You are completely worthy of honor and praise. Forgive me for the times I've tried to elevate myself at the expense of others. Keep me humble and honor me in Your own way and time.

WE SEEK TO PRAISE GOD

*But you are a chosen people, a royal priesthood,
a holy nation, God's special possession, that you
may declare the praises of him who called you
out of darkness into his wonderful light.*

1 PETER 2:9

To begin the Lord's Prayer, God's Son teaches us to pray, "Our Father in heaven, hallowed be your name, your kingdom come, your will be done, on earth as it is in heaven" (Matthew 6:9–10).

Everything about heaven is holy, honored, sanctified, consecrated, and sacred. That's because it's filled with God's hallowed presence.

Imagine joining Isaiah or John when they suddenly find themselves in heaven before God's throne. What would you see, hear, and feel in such a hallowed place?

Seraphim actively praising the Lord, saying, "Holy, holy, holy is the LORD Almighty; the whole earth is full of his glory" (Isaiah 6:3).

Other creatures praising the Lord, saying, " 'Holy, holy, holy is the Lord God Almighty,' who was, and is, and is to come" (Revelation 4:8).

Twenty-four elders praising the Lord by saying, "You are worthy, our Lord and God, to receive glory and honor and power, for you created all things, and by your will they were created and have their being" (Revelation 4:11).

Millions of angels praising the Lord, saying, "Worthy is the Lamb, who was slain, to receive power and wealth and wisdom and strength and honor and glory and praise!" (Revelation 5:12).

Billions of creatures praising the Lord, saying, "To him who sits on the throne and to the Lamb be praise and honor and glory and power, for ever and ever!" (Revelation 5:13).

To praise our heavenly Father here on earth prepares us for our greatest moments before God in heaven. Do it often!

God, indeed, to You be all glory, honor, and praise on earth as in heaven.

WE KEEP THE FAITH

*Christ can bring you to God, holy and pure
and without blame. This is for you if you
keep the faith. You must not change from
what you believe now. You must not leave
the hope of the Good News you received.*

COLOSSIANS 1:22–23 NLV

The overriding theme from Matthew to Revelation isn't how the world is going to end. Instead, it's how *your life* is going to end. The question is: Will you keep the faith and have a godly legacy? The answer is found in three biblical truths.

First, when we trust God, it's a slow process of coming to more and more faith in Him. There's no such thing as instant spiritual maturity. We all go through struggles, doubts, failures, and repentance before we come to the place of readily saying yes to God's Word and His will for our lives.

Second, it's often in the most difficult times that

we really grow in our faith. Not that we have to look for trouble. God's desire is to make us men who know how to go through trials and temptations, and know how to keep on keeping on, until the fruit of His Spirit is formed in us—godly character that hopes in God, no matter what the circumstances.

Third, God Himself deepens our faith in Him. The Bible speaks of many levels of faith: no faith, weak in faith, little faith, lack of faith, faith, growing faith, more faith, firm in faith, strong in faith, excelling in faith, and full of faith. We don't have to worry about generating more faith ourselves. Instead, scripture urges us to focus our faith on the ultimate reference point of the universe and of reality—God Himself.

We are made in His image. We draw our power for living from His Spirit. We keep the faith.

God, thank You for the gift of growing faith. I'm a work in progress and I yield my will and ways to Your Spirit. Help me to keep the faith, and to encourage other believers to do so as well.

WE SEEK THE BEST

But without faith it is impossible to please him: for he that cometh to God must believe that he is, and that he is a rewarder of them that diligently seek him.
<small>HEBREWS 11:6 KJV</small>

God is absolutely supreme. No one else even scratches the surface of His wisdom, power, and holiness. The apostle Paul expressed this truth to the polytheistic people of Athens, who filled their city with shrines to various false gods and even installed an altar "to an unknown God." Here's what Paul said about that: "You are ignorant of the very thing you worship—and this is what I am going to proclaim to you. The God who made the world and everything in it is the Lord of heaven and earth and does not live in temples built by human hands. And he is not served by human hands, as if he needed anything. Rather, he himself gives everyone life and breath and everything else. From one man he made all the nations, that they should inhabit the whole earth; and he marked out their appointed times in history and the boundaries of their lands. God did this so that they would seek him and perhaps reach out for him and find him, though he is not far from any one of us" (Acts 17:23–27).

Made in God's image, human beings long to worship. . . but marred by sin, we often worship the wrong things. In His kindness, this "unknown God" makes Himself approachable through His Son, Jesus Christ. God knows that He—the Trinity of Father, Son, and Holy Spirit—is the absolute best that any man could aspire to. And God makes Himself available to anyone who will humbly acknowledge Jesus Christ as Lord.

Our greatest quest, our seeking of the very best, is the pursuit of God Himself. Nothing else will ultimately satisfy. Nothing else will even come close.

God, thank You for bringing me to Yourself by Your grace through faith in Jesus Christ. Thank You for also saving others I know and love. Help me sense others who may be seeking You and Your best so I can point them to You.

WE BELIEVE THE BEST

Therefore, if anyone is in Christ, the new creation
has come: The old has gone, the new is here!
2 CORINTHIANS 5:17

By saying "we believe the best," we're not encouraging an unrealistic, Pollyanna-style approach to humanity. People are sinful and in need of salvation. Apart from Jesus, they (and *we*) are mean, selfish, and destructive. We shouldn't believe people are better than they truly are. . .but we must believe that God can change them.

God sees the potential in every person He's created. He wants every human being, who bears the stamp of His image, to be *re*-created by accepting the finished work of Jesus Christ and becoming a temple of the Holy Spirit (1 Corinthians 3:16 and 6:19). Nobody is beyond God's reach. Consider the zealous persecutor of Christians, Saul, who became the even-more-zealous Christian missionary Paul (Acts 9). Or the thief on the cross who began by mocking Jesus but died with the expectation of heaven (Matthew 27:44 and Luke 23:39-43).

And with those who are already brothers, let's be sure we give everyone a fair shake. Don't ever forget Jesus' words:

> *"Do not judge, or you too will be judged. For in the same way you judge others, you will be judged, and with the measure you use, it will be measured to you. Why do you look at the speck of sawdust in your brother's eye and pay no attention to the plank in your own eye? How can you say to your brother, 'Let me take the speck out of your eye,' when all the time there is a plank in your own eye? You hypocrite, first take the plank out of your own eye, and then you will see clearly to remove the speck from your brother's eye."*
> MATTHEW 7:1-5

God believed the best about you. Honor Him by viewing others through the same lens.

Father in heaven, where would I be today if You hadn't saved me? I thank You for making me part of Your family. May I view everyone else as a true or potential brother or sister.

WE WANT ALL PEOPLE TO REPENT

*The Lord is not slow in keeping his promise,
as some understand slowness. Instead he
is patient with you, not wanting anyone to
perish, but everyone to come to repentance.*

2 PETER 3:9

"Jesus wept." Did you know this appears in the Gospels *twice*? The second "Jesus wept" appears in John 11:35, after Lazarus of Bethany died. This shows that God weeps over the deaths of good, godly men. (Psalm 116:15 and Acts 7:55-60 provide a glimpse of God's strong concern over the deaths of His people).

The first "Jesus wept" (at least, a form of it) appears in Luke 19:41: "As he approached Jerusalem and saw the city, he wept over it." This indicates that God weeps ahead of time over the rigidly unrepentant, even before their deaths (so did His prophets: Isaiah 15:5, 16:9, 22:4-5, Jeremiah 9:1, 9:10, 13:17, and

Lamentations 1:16 and 2:11).

Conversely, all of heaven celebrates when one sinner comes to repentance (Luke 15:7, 10). We should too!

While she repeatedly kissed Jesus' feet, a repentant woman kept weeping (Luke 7:38). This was in the home of a Pharisee named Simon, who judged both the woman and Jesus. As God's Son, of course, Jesus knew the Pharisee's thoughts, so He told a quick parable, rebuked the man, and told the woman that her sins were forgiven. That provoked even more criticism of Jesus, who ignored it and went on to tell the woman, "Your faith has saved you; go in peace" (Luke 7:50).

What a great picture of God's desire that no one should perish, but that all should come to repentance. This idea is found throughout scripture (Isaiah 48:9, Jeremiah 36:3, Ezekiel 18:23, 18:32, 33:11, Jonah 3:10, Matthew 18:14, 1 Timothy 2:3–4, and 2 Peter 3:9).

God's heart is for the lost. As men made in His image, our heart should be for the lost too. Let's love them, pray for them, and share the good news of Jesus Christ with all who will listen.

God, thank You for celebrating when one sinner repents. Please use me to bring many other sinners into Your family!

WE GIVE GOOD GIFTS

*Give the gifts that are right and
good, and trust in the Lord.*
PSALM 4:5 NLV

As you have seen throughout this book, we can reflect God's image in dozens of ways. Those ways include as we work, create, provide, and protect; as we love, teach, confront, and forgive; and as we guide, help, encourage, and sacrifice.

We also reflect God's image as we celebrate, cherish, clothe, and comfort; as we enjoy, feed, give, and honor; and as we pray, provide, speak, and treasure.

As we reflect God's image, *we* are blessed, *others* are blessed, and the *world* is influenced for good and for God's glory, honor, and praise. What's more, over these past three months, you have probably deepened your appreciation for who God made you to be.

There's nothing more exciting, invigorating, and fulfilling than becoming more like your Lord and

Savior, and more fully owning your identity as "Made by God in His Image."

To experience the promised smiles, joy, and even fun, please don't put this book on a shelf—give it to a family member or friend. Tell him what this study has meant to you. Then challenge him to read one daily devotional for the next hundred days. Offer to take him out for breakfast, coffee, or lunch. . .and even promise a reward for staying the course.

As God has blessed you, now bless someone else. Your family member or friend will be glad. And so will you!

God, indeed, You have blessed me. Now,
I promise to bless someone else. Put someone
on my mind. Then give me the opportunity
to see him—and give him this book. Amen!

MORE GREAT DEVOTIONS FOR MEN

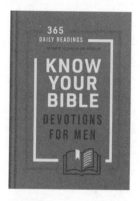

Inspired by the 3-million-copy bestseller, *Know Your Bible Devotions for Men* provides 365 readings focusing on important verses of scripture, offering background, insight, and encouraging takeaways. You'll get a fascinating overview of all 66 books—an excellent primer if you're new to God's Word, and a helpful refresher if you're already familiar with scripture.

Hardcover / 978-1-63609-206-5 / $16.99